I0138983

Periphrases in Medieval English

STUDIES IN ENGLISH MEDIEVAL LANGUAGE AND LITERATURE

Edited by Jacek Fisiak

Advisory Board:
John Anderson (Methoni, Greece), Ulrich Busse (Halle),
Olga Fischer (Amsterdam), Marcin Krygier (Poznań),
Roger Lass (Cape Town), Peter Lucas (Cambridge),
Donka Minkova (Los Angeles), Akio Oizumi (Kyoto),
Katherine O'Brien O'Keeffe (UC Berkeley, USA),
Matti Rissanen (Helsinki), Hans Sauer (Munich),
Liliana Sikorska (Poznań), Jeremy Smith (Glasgow),
Jerzy Wełna (Warsaw)

Vol. 54

PETER LANG

Michiko Ogura

Periphrases in Medieval English

PETER LANG

Bibliographic Information published by the Deutsche Nationalbibliothek
The Deutsche Nationalbibliothek lists this publication in the Deutsche Nationalbibliografie; detailed bibliographic data is available in the internet at http://dnb.d-nb.de.

Library of Congress Cataloging-in-Publication Data
A CIP catalog record for this book has been applied for at the Library of Congress.

ISSN 1436-7521
ISBN 978-3-631-75680-5 (Print)
E-ISBN 978-3-631-76275-2 (E-PDF)
E-ISBN 978-3-631-76276-9 (EPUB)
E-ISBN 978-3-631-76277-6 (MOBI)
DOI 10.3726/b14460

© Peter Lang GmbH
Internationaler Verlag der Wissenschaften
Berlin 2018
All rights reserved.

Peter Lang – Berlin · Bern · Bruxelles · New York ·
Oxford · Warszawa · Wien

All parts of this publication are protected by copyright. Any utilisation outside the strict limits of the copyright law, without the permission of the publisher, is forbidden and liable to prosecution. This applies in particular to reproductions, translations, microfilming, and storage and processing in electronic retrieval systems.

This publication has been peer reviewed.

www.peterlang.com

To Jacek Fisiak

Contents

Preface

From about 1980 onwards many books and articles have been published on Old and Middle English syntax, as Mitchell's *Old English Syntax* is a representative. Owing to the development of technological devices, the making of web corpora has accelerated the use of the great amount of data in this field, and the limited number of medieval texts has become a strong point of digitalising the data. Many early manuscripts have been made available on the screen, which has enliven the discussion on the original texts without turning pages by our own hands. The most striking change has occurred in dictionaries. The 3rd edition of the *Oxford English Dictionary* is now on the website and the data can be updated whenever necessary; the difference between the paper version of the 2nd edition of *OED* and the digitalised *OED3* is now quite noticeable.

I started writing on Old English syntax from 1974 and enjoyed finding examples of a particular construction which was earlier than the first quotation in *OED*. But now almost all my findings are cited clearly in *OED3*, *MED* or *DOE* Web Corpus. Though the completion of *DOE* as a dictionary is unpredictable at this stage, we have the whole remaining data of Old English texts based on, and updated constantly, the *Microfiche Concordance* preceding this computer era. As both linguists and philologists have started using the *DOE*, *OED3* and *MED* data, citations from each specific edition is now used only in discussions or critical comments as variant readings. We should be mindful of looking at these alternative readings or possible choices, without ignoring them. In this monograph I shall give the dictionary data first so that everyone may notice what dictionaries say admitting the results of investigations in recent years, and then add past and present opinions of studies in this field. The important thing, I think, is to show the tendency found in the history of English — the tendency of using various periphrastic constructions throughout the language history so as to make the records, translations, and literary works to be readable, as well as people make the speech communicative. Old English data is left for us in the process of making the language periphrastic, i.e. the periphrastic tendency had already started, and it became obvious in the transitional period, even though the data was scarce, because we find the syntactic shift from Anglo-Saxon to 'English', accelerated by the morphological change. The tendency of using periphrases has continued even after the medieval period, which gives a variety of expressions in the English language.

Acknowledgements are due to the librarians of the British Library, London, Bodleian library, Oxford, and Parker Library and University Library, Cambridge, for letting me investigate manuscripts of the Gospels: MSS Auct.D.2.19, Bodley 441, Corpus Christi College Cambridge 140, Cotton Neor D.iv, Cotton Otho c.i. (vol.1), Eng.B.b.C.2, Hatton 38, and Royal I.A xiv. My studies on medieval English for these thirty years or so have been done by the generous grants from the Japan Society for the Promotion of Science, the British Council and the British Academy.

Summer 2017

Table of Abbreviations

Abbreviated titles of the texts examined are shown in Select Bibliography.

OE	Old English	eOE	early Old English
ME	Middle English	lOE	late Old English
MnE	Modern English	eME	early Middle English
PDE	Present-Day English	lME	late Middle English
L	Latin		
OF	Old French		
ON	Old Norse		
OHG	Old High German		
OS	Old Saxon		
Goth	Gothic		
Gmc	Germanic		
PIE	Proto-Indo-European		

S	subject
V	verb
O	object
Aux	auxiliary
Inf	infinitive
Part	particle
past ptc	past participle
pres ptc	present participle
V^{imp}	verb in the imperative
Conj	conjunction
Dem	demonstrative
Adj	adjective
Adv	adverb
Prep	preposition

Chapter 1 Introduction

English as a descendent of the Germanic family of language lacked some morphological verb forms from the start. When the Anglo-Saxons wrote down to record their language, they made a good use of periphrastic expressions with auxiliaries. If a particular form is enough for one syntactic function, a grammar book of that language could be written in a simple and straightforward way. As a language, Old English was (i) incomplete in the tense system, while (ii) case endings were still reliable; (iii) its word order was systematically different from what we have in the Present-Day English (hereafter PDE); (iv) lexemes were chiefly Germanic, with a few Latin to be understood, and (v) their shades of meaning were mostly dissimilar to those of PDE. It can be said, therefore, that we have a partial knowledge of Old English, owing to the limited data left with us.

When the Proto-Indo-European (hereafter PIE) language is reconsidered in comparison, it had eight cases: nominative, vocative, genitive, dative, instrumental, locative, ablative, and accusative, six of which was left to Latin and four (or five in a few forms) to Germanic (hereafter Gmc). PIE had three genders: masculine, feminine and neuter; three numbers: singular, dual and plural, all of which descended to Gmc. It had two voices: active and medio-passive; the latter became passive in Gmc, and its function survived in syntactic constructions of reflexive and 'impersonal' in Old English. PIE had four moods: indicative, optative, conjunctive and imperative; conjunctive was later called subjunctive, which subsequently covered optative (e.g. PDE *God save the queen* or *May Christ forbid us*) and hautative (e.g. OE *uton gan*, PDE *Let's go*). PIE had three tenses: present, aorist and perfect; Gmc had two tense forms: present and preterit; this fact caused Old English to seek for the devices of representing perfect, future, progressive (and/or inceptive).

Another problem which we encounter when reading Old English is word order. As Andrew (1940) states, the common order was SVO, then the conjunctive order, Conj S (O) V and demonstrative order, Dem VS(O), and the emphatic order like OSV or OVS. Such misnomers given by theoretical linguists as OV Language and Verb Second were born by the fact that SVO was normal in the principal clause but SOV was mostly found in the subordinate clause; but owing to the correlative construction, modern readers cannot distinguish which is which, when examples were given in an improper length. We must admit another fact that we are not always sure which element in a sentence is emphasised when we face an unusual order.

When early English (Old and Middle English) and later English (Modern and Present-Day English) are compared, the following features can be identified as the first and the final stages of a historical shift.

early English	*later English*
correlative	relative
--------→	
asyndetic (or paratactic)	hypotactic
co-ordinate	subordinate
þæt-clause	infinitive
---------→	
subjunctive	auxiliary

This process should be called a "shift" rather than a "change" because the final stage was already found in a few examples of early English. Correlative constructions, e.g. *þa ...þa..., þonne...þonne..., þær...þær...*, etc., were typical in Old English and useful for combining a principal clause and a subordinate clause. In fact they often lead to an ambiguity owing to the same form, that is, difficult to identify which is 'then' and which is 'when', when SV and VS orders were not reliable enough. We learn that Ælfric often used *þa þa ... þa ...* 'when ... then ...', though not a widespread devise. From Middle English onwards, the '*if ... then ...*' type of combinations developed. Asyndetic means a *veni, vidi, vici* type of expression, often found in Old English verse texts, which can also be called paratactic. Co-ordination is exemplified by a sequence of *and*-clauses, which is a typically medieval syntax, often recognised as a biblical expression. Later constructions, relative, hypotactic and subordinate constructions, were already seen in Old English, but correlative, asyndetic and co-ordinate constructions were so characteristic that modern readers often get foreign images in Old English syntax.

14

þæt had a wider function than *that* in PDE. A *þæt*-clause could be nominal, adjectival, adverbial, relative, meaning 'that', 'so that', 'now that', 'in order that', 'for the reason that', 'that which', etc. As it was often used to translate Latin conjunctions, *hit is us neod þæt* ... was more natural in Old English than *it is necessary for us to do*.... Subjunctive forms were so useful that modal auxiliaries were, though used, not always necessary.

In auxiliaries that I discuss here are included modal auxiliaries, *beon/wesan/weorðan, habban, don* and some other verbs which take an infinitive. It seems, therefore, better for me to explain the earlier use of *beon* by quoting part of *OES* § 659, in which Mitchell refers to the remarks of Mustanoja and Campbell: "Mustanoja (p. 583) says that 'while the principal function of *wesan* is to express a state prevailing generally or at the time of speaking, that of *beon* is to express future or iterative activity'.

> The distinction of the pres. indic. tenses *eom* and *beo* is fairly well preserved in OE: *beo* expresses what is (*a*) an invariable fact, e.g. *ne bið swylc cwenlic þeaw* 'such is not a queenly custom' [*Beow*. 1940], or (*b*) the future, e.g. *ne bið þe wilna gad* 'you will have no lack of pleasures' [id. 660], or (*c*) iterative extension into the future, e.g. *biþ storma gehwylc aswefed* 'every storm is always allayed' (i.e. on all occasions of the flight of the Phoenix, past and to come) [*Phoen*. 185–6]; *eom* expresses a present state provided its continuance is not especially regarded, e.g. *wlitig is se wong* 'the plain is beautiful'."

I notice some different sense of *oft* with *beon* in *Phoenix*: *Phoen* 11 *Ðær bið oft open eadgum togeanes / onhliden hleoþra wyn, heofonrices duru* 'There the door of the heavenly kingdom, the joy of harmony, will be open and unlocked at all times against the blessed.' The word *oft* here may mean not 'often' but 'at all times' or 'again and again.'

Explanations of *OED3* and *DOE* should be compared first.[1] In *OED3* **be** v. under IV. With participles and infinitives, as an auxiliary and forming compound tenses, the following explanations are found. (Dates in square brackets are mine.)

---

1   In *DOE* headwords, Matti Kilpiö is responsible for *beon* and *habban*. For the differences of explanation in *OED* and *DOE* see Ogura (2011b), though at that time *OED3* was not available and the information became now partly archaic.

16. With past participle.
    a. In transitive verbs, forming the passive voice.
        (a) In simple tenses, imperative, and infinitive of the auxiliary. [found from eOE]
        (b) In the present participle passive. [1422–]
        (c) In progressive tenses of the auxiliary, forming the progressive passive. [(1667) 1772–]
    b. In intransitive verbs, forming perfect tenses; in later use chiefly with verbs of motion such as *come, go, rise, set, fall, arrive, depart, grow*, etc., expressing a condition or state attained at the time of speaking, rather than the action of reacing it, e.g. 'the sun is set', 'our guests are gone', 'Babylon is fallen', 'the children are all grown up'.
    Now largely replaced by *have* following the pattern of transitive verbs: see HAVE *v.* VI.
    eOE *Anglo-Saxon Chron.* (Parker) anno 893 *Wæs Hæsten þa þær cumen mid his herge.*

17. With the present participle, forming progressive tenses.
    From the 15th to the early 20th cent., the auxiliary itself could be used in the present participle (e.g. 'being walking', 'being making').
    a. With active meaning (until about 14th cent. still with some of the properties of a copula and participial adjective).
    eOE *Anglo-Saxon Chron.* (Parker) anno 855 *Æþelwulf cyning .. was xii monaþ wuniende.*
    b. With passive meaning. Now *arch.* and *rare* except in *nothing doing* at DO *v.*
    With the construction seen in 'the ark was building' compare the earlier constructions exemplified by 'the ark was in building' (see IN *prep.* 11d) and 'the ark was a-building' (see A *prep.* 12.). [a1400 (a1325) *Cursor Mundi* (Vesp.) l. 26813–]

Concerning OE examples, a comparison between this explanation and that of *DOE* seems necessary. Under **bēon** B.13. combinations of copula and agent noun, the combination best translated into ModE by a single verb, *DOE* gives an example from prose Boethius: *Bo* 34.84.21 *ac we sculon bion geþafan þætte se God sie earla þinga betst* ('we must consent that'; cf. BOETH. Cons. Phil. pr.3.10.13 *sed hunc esse rerum omnium praecellentissimum dignissime confitemur*). It is true that "the combination best translated into ModE by a single verb", but this kind of construction is not so rare in OE (e.g. *beon bana* 'be a killer', any influence from Old Norse?) and the fact should be mentioned.

16

The verb *have* has relation to many periphrastic expressions with other auxiliaries. As a verb of possession it was synonymous with a preterite-present verb *agan*, as a rendering of Latin future tense it could be used as a future auxiliary, and make a combination with past participle of the transitive verb to form the prefect, and was used with a *to*-infinitive to show obligation and became synonymous with *should* or *must*. The early example of *have to* 'to be under obligation' is attested in the early thirteenth century and quoted in *MED* (**haven** v. 11. (b)): *a1225 (c1200) Vices & V. (1) (Stw 34) 75/6 Alle ðo þing ðe ðu hauest te donne, do it mid ræde*. The '*habban* + *to*-infinitive' construction was, however, found in West Saxon Gospels where the glosses produce '*beon* + present participle':[2]

(1) Mt 20.22 [potestis bibere calicem quem ego **bibiturus sum**][3]
    Li: magage drinca calic ðone **ic drincende beom** ł drinca **willo**
  Ru1:   magon git ðene kælic drncan þe **ic drincande beom**
 WSCp: mage gyt drincan þone calic ðe **ic to drincenne hæbbe**
WycEV: Mowen ȝe drynke the cuppe that **I am to drynke?**
   AV: Are ye able to drinke of the cup that **I shall drink of**,

It is not easy to interpret the double gloss in Lindisfarne; how to reproduce the futurity is probably the point, and '*beon* + present participle' was the

---

2 *Habban to* can be attested in, for example, *Lk(Li)* 23.17 [*habebat dimittere eis*] *hæfeð ł hæfde to forgeafanne him* and *ChronE* 1129.7 *Cristendome hæfdon to begemen ⁊ to locen*, where the object of the infinitive co-occurs. This construction is not the origin of *have to* 'have something to do' and often seen in such phrases as 'have ears to hear (*Mt(WSCp)* 11.15, *Mk(WSCp)* 4.9, 4.23, *Lk(WSCp)* 14.34), 'have a long story to tell' (*Or 2* 8.53.4) and 'have permission to trade' (*Gen* 42.34). In *MED* **haven** (v.) 11. the example from *Peterborough Chronicle* is quoted first under (a) To have (sth. in order to do sth. with it), and under (b) to be under obligation (to do sth.), have (to do sth.) the first example is *a1225(c1220) Vices & V.(1) (Stw 34) 75/6*. Precisely it should be (b) that is the direct origin of PDE *have to*.

3 Throughout this book I follow *DOE* and *MED* in the abbreviated titles. As for the examples from the Gospels and the Psalter, I use each edition in the Selected Bibliography with abbreviated titles. Other editions in the Selected Bibliography (without abbreviated titles) are those I consult on manuscript variants, comments, and notes and glossaries. Modern English translations are put after all the Old English examples and some Middle English ones. Translations are mine, unless otherwise stated. Boldface in the examples is mine to highlight the words or phrases in question.

first choice and '*willan* + infinitive' was the second. Rushworth 1 chose the first. In the free translation of the West Saxon version, however, the choice was '*habban* + *to*-infinitive'. The Wycliffite shows '*be* + *to*-infinitve' and *AV* '*shall* + infinitive'. *RSV* has *Are you able to drink the cup that I am to drink*. We cannot definitely say that *Li willo* suggested the futurity rather than the volition, or *WSCp to drincenne hæbbe* meant the futurity or obligation, neither. But this is how the Anglo-Saxons tried to develop their syntactic patterns which they did not use so often in their daily speech.

Here in this monograph I refer to my books and articles for additional data. In Chapter 2 (*beon/habban* + past ptc) I refer to Ogura (1996b, 1997a, 1997c, 2002a, 2002b, 2009), in Chapter 3 (*beon/wesan/weorðan* + past ptc) to Ogura (1982), in Chapter 4 (*man*-periphrasis) to Ogura (1990b), in Chapter 5 (*beon/wesan* + pres ptc) to Ogura (2014), in Chapter 6 (*onginan/beginnan* + Inf) to Ogura (1997b), in Chapter 8 (*don* periphrasis) to Ogura (2003a, 2003d), in Chapter 9 (*uton* + Inf) to Ogura (2000), in Chapter 11 (modal auxiliaries) to Ogura (2007b), in Chapter 12 (double modals) to Ogura (1993c, 1998a), in Chapter 13 ('impersonals' and 'reflexives') to Ogura (1986a, 1988c, 1989a, 1989b, 1990a, 1991c, 2001a, 2001b, 2003c, 2004a, 2005a, 2007a, 2012a, 2012b, 2013b, 2016, 2017), in Chapter 14 ('Prep + noun' and verb-adverb combination) to Ogura (1991a, 1991e, 1992, 1993b, 1995, 2006a, 2006b, 2008a, 2008b, 2010, 2018), in Chapter 15 (periphrases died out) to Ogura (1984, 1986b, 1987, 1988a, 1988b), and periphrases in general to Ogura (1991b, 1991c, 1993a, 1994, 1996a, 1998b, 2008c, 2008d, 2011a, 2013a, 2013c). For the basic studies I use, see also Select Bibliography.

Chapter 2 *beon/habban* + past participle

2.1. Dictionary Data and Additional Data

OED3 has the following explanation in **have** *v.* under the signification VI. As an auxiliary verb, used with the past participle of another verb to form the perfect.

> The *have*-perfect in English apparently arose as a reanalysis of uses such as *I have my work done* 'I have my work in a done or finished condition' (see sense 7b); the complement *done* was reinterpreted as part of the verb phrase, a process which was reinforced by a lack of fixed word order and the possible transposition of object and participle, i.e. *I have done my work*. This development appears to have largely taken place before the written record. Even in early Old English, in the majority of examples with transitive verbs the past participle is not inflected to agree with the object. Despite occasional ambiguity, there are few Old English examples in which the past participle must be regarded as a complement rather than as part of a perfect construction.
>
> In Old English, the *have*-perfect is not only established with transitive verbs, but also with intransitive verbs expressing action or occurrence, while the perfect of intransitive verbs expressing change of state or position is usually formed with *be* (BE *v.* 16b). From Middle English onwards the perfect with *have* gradually becomes more common in these verbs, and is the predominant form by the early 19th cent., except in contexts where the focus is on resultant state (for example, *she is gone* is still typically used to express state, while *she has gone* expresses action; such usage is now, however, quite limited). In early Middle English the *have*-perfect also extends to verbs denoting ongoing states or conditions, and to the verb *to be*.

Under 30. With a transitive verb, *OED3* chooses good Old English examples which give proofs of the above explanation: eOE (Kentish) *Charter: Lufu to Christ Church, Canterbury* (Sawyer 1197) in F. E. Hamer *Sel.Eng. Hist.Docs.9th & 10th Cent.* (1914) 8 *Đet ic beboden hebbe an ðisem gewrite*, OE Ælfric *Catholic Homilies: 1st Ser.* (Royal) (1997) x.258 *þin geleafa hæfð þe gehæled* [OE *Blickling Homilies þe hæfþ gehælene*; L. (Vulgate) *te salvum fecit*], OE *Old Eng. Hexateuch: Gen.* (Claud.) xlii.36 *Bearnleasne ge habbað me gedonne* [L. *me esse fecistis*]. Under 31. a. With an intransitive verb denoting an action or occurrence, the first example is: eOE KING ÆLFRED tr. Gregory *Pastoral Care* (Hatton) (1871) xxvi.185 *Đonne mon ðnne ongiete ðæt he ryhte gedemed hæbbe* [L. *cum rectam sententiam quasi in alterum protulerint*], while b. With an intransitive verb denoting a change from one state or position to another, as *come, depart, go grow*, etc., c. With an intransitive verb denoting an ongoing state or condition, as *continue, live, remain, stay*, etc. and d. With *been*, past participle of BE *v.*, the first examples are from *Lambeth Homilies*, *Trinity Homilies*, and *Vespasian Homilies*, all from the transitional period.

As has been seen in the explanation of *OED3*, a kind of rule was seen in early English, i.e.

beon/wesan + past participle of an intransitive verb
habban + past participle of a transitive verb

which is not a strict rule at all, but has been accepted in general. I have already found examples of past participle of verbs of motion which co-occur with *beon* and *habban* in Old English.[1] In the following examples, *wæs gefaren* and *hæfde gefaren* in *Orosius* may mean much the same,[2] while *wæs gefaren* and *hæfdon gefaren* in *ChronE* were different, i.e. in the former combination the verb is used intransitively but in the latter transitively.

(2) Or 4 8.100.5
se **wæs** on Sicilium mid firde **gefaren**
'who had marched in Sicily with the troop'

(3) Or 4 10.104.29
Þa Scipia **hæfde gefaren** to ðære niwan byrig Cartaina, þe mon nu Cordofa hætt,
'When Scipio had marched to the new city Carthage, which is now called Córdoba'

(4) ChronE (Irvine) 1100.38
forþan þe he **wæs** ut of þis lande **gefaren** for þan mycelan unrihte þe se cyng Willelm him dyde.
'because he was gone out of this land on account of the great injustice which King William had done to him'

(5) ChronE (Irvine) 1048.31
⁊ Eustatius ætbærst mid feawum mannum ⁊ gewende ongean to þam cynge ⁊ cydde be dæle hu hi **gefaren hæfdon**,
'and Eustace escaped with a few men and went back to the king and made a partial statement how they had experienced'

---

1 See Ogura (1996b).
2 In example (3) *gefaran* may mean 'to make an attack (to)'; see *DOE* **gefaran** 1.A.2.a., for which definitions I am responsible.

As to the development of *beon* and *habban* as perfect auxiliaries, Traugott (1972: 93–94) gives the following examples for comparison. She states the past participle with an inflectional ending *-e* as "adjectival" and without an ending as "perfective".

(6) Or 5 4.118.5
   <Crassuse> **wæron** monege cyningas of monegum landum to fultume **cumene**.
   'Many kings had come to Craccus from many lands as help.'
   'to Craccus were many kings … as help come' (by Traugott)

(7) Or 2 5.47.19
   Hie **wæron cumen** Leoniðan to fultume
   'They had come to Leonitha as help.'
   'they were come to-Leonitha as help = they had come to help Leonitha.' (by Traugott)

(8) BoProem 1.6³
   ⁊ þeah ða þas boc <**hæfde**> **geleornode** ⁊ of lædene to engliscum spelle **gewende**,
   'and though when (he) had learned these books and translated to English prose from Latin'
   'when (he) those books had in-a-state-of-learnedness' (by Traugott)

(9) CPLetWærf 36
   ða wundrade ic swiðe swiðe ðara godena wiotona ðe giu wæron giond An-gelcynn, ⁊ ða bec eallæ be fullan **geliornod hæfdon**,
   'then I wondered very much at those good and wise men who had been all over England, and had learned all these books completely'
   'of-wise-men who … those books completely learned had' (by Traugott)

and I add examples of *gebunden(ne)*, which Traugott mentions without examples. In (10) there is another combination *asungen hæfde*, where *lioð* is a noun and the past participle has to have no inflectional ending; *me* can be either accusative or dative, but the inflected form *gebundenne* tells that it is accusative. In the same way, *gebunden* agrees with *feond* (masculine accusative singular), and it is not certain if the uninflected form suggests the "perfective" function.

---

3 *Hæfde* was emended from MS. B *hæfe*. Traugott omitted & *þeah* before *þa* in her example.

(10) Bo 22.50.8

> ða se Wisdom þa ðis lioð **asungen hæfde**, þa **hæfde** he me **gebundenne** mid þære wynsumnesse his sanges,
> 'When Philosophy had sung this song, then (s)he had bound me with the delightfulness of his (her) song'

(11) ÆCHom I, 31 441.63

> Ic **hæbbe gebunden** þone feond þe hi drehte. ⁊ ge gyt hi ondrædað?
> 'I have bound the fiend who trouled her, and yet you fear her?'

In the two manuscripts of the late thirteenth century Laȝamon, '*be* + past participle' and a simple present or preterite verb form appear as variants.

	Calig.	Otho
291	Þa þe time com	Þo þe time icome was
1468–9	þat his blod & his brain	þat his blod and his braȝen
	ba weoren to-dascte.	boþe vt þraste.
1863	þat folc cō to sonne⁴	þat folk was igadered
3522	He cumeð for neode	He his icome for neode
9214	Þe kæisere hine wrædde	Þe kaiser him iwarþ wroþ
10934–5	ȝet ne com Maximien	ȝet nas Maximan
	neuere to Rome aȝen.	noht icome to Rome aȝein.
13080	þat þu ært icumen her	þat þou euere come her
13791–2	þreo scipen gode	þreo sipes gode
	comen mid þan flode.	i-come were mid þan flode.

There also appear '*have* + past participle' and a simple verb as variants.

	Calig.	Otho
604–5	þat Brutus hefde þa men	þat Brut*us* hafde þe men
	þe he mid fihte biwō.	þat mid fihte he hafde awonne.
758	al swa Brutus him hefde itaiht	ase Brut*us* hine lerede
14194–5	þ þu æi hæhne burhȝe	þat þou eni heh borh
	hæðene monne habbe bi-tæht.	Heþene man bi-takest.

There are two examples, in which '*be* + past participle' and '*have* + past participle' occur as manuscript variants, concerning the perfect and passive constructions.

(12) Laȝ 8818

> C: **i-numen weoren** [weore?] ure kingeˑ & his Bruttes alle aqualde.
> O: **inome hadde ibeo** þe kingˑ and his men acwelled.
> 'our king had been taken, and all his Britons killed'

---

4   *Sonne* should be read as *somne*.

(13) Laȝ 21649–50

    C: and ȝif Ardur [Arður?] **neore** þe rader [raðer?] þenne **weoren** Houwel
    inumen.

    O: and ȝef he **nadde** þe raþer **bi-come:** Howel **hadde bi nome** [be inome?]
    'and if Arthur had not arrived the earlier, then Howel had been taken'

Habban, a verb of possession as a main verb, was used as a perfect auxiliary
and a future auxiliary in glossing Latin, e.g.

(14) Mk 11.6 [qui dixerunt eis sicut **praeceperat** illis *iesu*s et dimiserunt eis]

    Li: ða ðe cuoeden him suæ **gehaten hæfde** him se *hæ*l*end* ⁊ *for*leorton him

  Ru2: ðaðe cwedun him swa **gihaten hæfde** hia ðe *hæ*l*end* ⁊ forleortun hine

 WSCp: þa cwædon hi; Swa se hælend unc **bead** ⁊ hi leton hi þa;

WycEV: And thei seiden to hem, as Jhesus **comaundide** to hem [LV: hem]; and
      thei leften hem.

    AV: And they said vnto them euen as Iesus **had commanded**: and they let
      them goe.

(15) Lk 23.17 [necesse autem **habebat dimittere** eis per diem festum unum]

    Li: ned-ðarf ðon*ne* **hæfeð** ǀ **hæfde to** *for*geafanne him ðerh ðone symbel-
      dæg enne ǀ an

  Ru2: ned-ðærfe ðonne **hæfeð to forgeofunne** him ðerh ðo*ne* symbeldæg enne

 WSCp: Niede he **sceolde** hi*m* **forgyfan** anne to hyra freols-dæge.

WycEV: Forsothe he **hadde** nede **to deliuere** to hem oon by the feeste day.

WycLV: But he **moste** nede **delyuer** to hem oon bi the feest dai.

    AV: For of necessitie hee **must release** one vnto them at the Feast.

As seen in (15), '*habban* + *to*-infinitive' could mean an obligation in the
future rather than a mere future, as a variant expression may include *sculan*
or 'must need'. A similar example is found in the *Peterborough Chronicle*.

(16) ChronE (Irvine) 1129.7

    Đa sone be þes kynges ræd ⁊ be his leue sende se ærcebiscop Willelm of
    Cantwarbyrig ofer eall Englaland ⁊ bead biscopes ⁊ abbotes ⁊ ærcedæcnes ⁊
    ealle þa priores, muneces ⁊ canonias þa wæron on ealle þa cellas on Engla-
    land, ⁊ æfter ealle þa þet Cristendome **hæfdon to begemen** ⁊ **to locen**, ⁊ þet
    hi scolden ealle cumen to Lundene at Michaeles messe ⁊ þær scolden sprecon
    of ealle Godes rihtes.

    'Then immediately by the king's counsel and by his leave William the arch-
    bishop of Canterbury sent all over England and commanded bishops, abbots,
    archdeacons, all the priors, monks and canons who were in all the cells in
    England, and then (commanded) all that they had to take care and look after
    the Christendom, and that they must come to London at Michaelmas and
    there must speak of all rights of God.'

2.2. Usefulness of the periphrasis

Because of the two-tense system inherited as a descendant of Germanic languages, Old English needed a devise of showing the detailed difference in tense. The '*beon/habban* + past participle' is a useful construction, along with the use of adverbs of time like *ær* and *nu giet*. The choice of *beon* and *habban* was necessary in Old English, when a verb could be used both transitively and intransitively according to contexts with some change of meaning. '*Beon* + past participle' construcions were kept in use up to late Modern English, especially with verbs denoting change.

Chapter 3 *beon/wesan/weorðan +* past participle

This chapter focuses on the passive construction, in contrast with the active one. A phenomenon can be expressed by the active or the passive, as long as the verb is used transitively. Thus the same thing can be reported as *ChronA* 1017 *Her Cnut wearð gecoran to kinge* 'In this year Cnut was chosen as king' and *ChronE* 1017 *Her on þisum geare feng Cnut cyning to eall Angel cynnes rice* 'In this year Cnut succeeded to all the kingdom of the Angles'. In Old English we have one single form of the passive *hatte*, but even this form may have alternative passive periphrasis *beon/wesan gehaten*.

3.1. Dictionary Data and Additional Data

OE *hatan* survived into Modern English, having various senses, 'to name', 'to command', 'to promise (which goes back to OE *gehatan > behatan*)' and 'to call oneself; to be called (OE *hatte, hatton*, besides *hateð, hatað*)'. In *OED3* has earlier examples for 'to promise': *Lk(Li)* (headings to readings) lxxiii [*promittit*] *heht*, *Orm* 4922 *þatt tatt icc het drihhtin*, *LaȝA* 11669 *ȝet ich wulle haten* [B: *hete*] *mare*, and for 'to be called': *CP* 58.445.33 *On ðæm bocum ðe hatton Apocalipsin*, *Or* 1 1.15.9 *Þa deor hi hatað hranas*, *Mt(WSCp)* 13.55 *Hu ne hatte* [L. *dicitur*] *hys modor Maria?*

The two manuscripts of Laȝamon's *Brut* show some contrasting choice of these expressions as follows.

	Calig.	Otho
219	Albe Lingoe wes ihaten	Albe Lingwe ihote
679	Anacletus wes ihaten	Anacletus ihote
1172	Gerion hehte þe preost	Gerion was ihote
1976	& his folk wes ihaten Sexuns	and cleopede his men Saxuns
2038	& Trinouant heo nemneden	and Trineavant hine hehte
2377	swa Locrin hine hefde ihaten	ase he was ihote
3885	Riwald wes ihaten	Riwald ihote
4643	& ich hatte Godlac	and ich hote Gutlac
7023	Ældolf men cleopeden þene king	Deldol was i-hote
9144	& þat scolde beon i-haten Hæled	and he solde hote: worlene Helare
11150	þe ældeste hæhte Leonin	þat þus were i-hote
11188	heo hehten hine forð riht anan	þat child was ihote

25

20794	Childric ihaten	þat Cheldrich his ihote
22471	Ælcus þe kīg wes ihatē	Alcus hehte þe king
26146	nu hit hæhte Munt Seint Myhhel	þat nou hatte Mont Seint Michel

Sometimes we see '*be* + adjective' and a verb in variation.

	Calig.	Otho
2478	þer he wes feie	þare he deaide
2569	þ he sone dæd wes	þat he solde deȝe
9214	Þe kæisere hine wrædde[1]	Þe kaiser him iwarþ wroþ
11899	& alle his beornen he wes leof	and alle hine lofuede
Cf. 22779	Þa duȝeðe wærð iwraððed	þat somme weren wel wroþ

(Ge)weorðan is said to be a passive auxiliary. In fact, it is used in the passive construction, in contrast with the active, as in (17). Since the verb has a sense 'to become', it can also be used to express 'be dead', as in (18), as well as *wesan*.

(17) Laȝ 1112
    C: heo wenden vt i wide sæ: þa wilde **wurðen** itemede.
    O: hii wenden vt in wilde [wide?] séé: þat þe wilde temieþ.
    'they went our in the wide sea; the wild (waves) were tamed (stilled)'

(18) Laȝ 11852–6[2]
    C: þær **wes** Caradoc **dæd**. þa hauede Mauric his sune: sorȝen inowe. nes þer nan oðer ræd: buten þe Mavric **iwærð dæd**.
    O: þar **was** Cradoc **dead**. so sori was his sone: þat he **deiȝede** eke.
    'there Cradoc was dead. Then Maurice his son had sorrow enough; there was no other misfortune but that Maurice was also dead (= should die).'

---

1 Read *wræðde*.
2 In Ogura (1982) I present the lexical field of *dead* which consists of four parts: I *dead* (i.e. be + adjective of the same etymon of the verb), II *fallen* or *dying* (be + past ptc or pres. ptc), III *lifeless* (i.e. with prefix *un-* or suffix *-less*), and IV *killed* (passive). When the Gospels and the alliterative poems of OE, OHG, OS and ON are compared, I get the following results. In the Gospels it is Part I that is predominant, Part IV is the second, except for Gothic, and seems to be wider after the medieval period in English. In alliterative poems, Part I is wider in OE but much the same as Part IV in OS and ON. Interestingly, there is no examples in Part II an OS and Part III in ON, which may tell the fondness and avoidance of one or the other element according to language. (Owing to the old editions I had to use at that time, the counting might not be appropriate. Here I give only percentages. See Ogura (1982: 16–17) in detail.)

Other variants which may concern with the choice of different voice, mood or style can be found in the following examples, when they are quoted in a longer context.

(19) Laȝ 6490
    C: he igrap his spere stronge: þer he pihte hit o þon londe.
    O: He grop his spere stronge: þar hit was ipiht in londe.
    'He grasped his strong spear, where he (it was) pitched in the land.'

(20) Laȝ 8951
    C: grið þer heo astalleden: & wel hit wes ihalden.
    O: griþ hii þare makede: and hit wel helde.
    'peace there they established, and it was kept well (and they kept it well)'

(21) Laȝ 15007
    C: & drinken half þat ilke win: þat heo heuede idon þer in.
    O: ād drong alf þat ilke win: þat was idon þar in.
    'and drink half of the same wine that she had put (that was put) therein'

(22) Laȝ 15349
    C: & al swa he idode: alse hit idemed was.
    O: and al so he dude: alse hii hit wolde.
    'and all so he did, as it was deemed (as they wished)'

Gospels in comparison

	Goth	Tatian	WS	Li	Wyc	Tyn
I	66.6%	74.5%	82.9%	90.3%	85.2%	80.7%
II	16.7%	6.4%	5.7%	2.2%	3.7%	1.8%
III	0	0	0	0	0	0
IV	16.7%	19.1%	11.4%	7.5%	11.1%	17.5%

Alliterative poems

	OS	OE	ON
I	47.4%	55.6%	41.2%
II	0	2.8%	15.7%
III	5.2%	22.2%	0
IV	47.4%	19.4%	43.1%

N. B. The texts I used for Goth was Bosworth and Waring (1888), for Tatian, Sievers (1892, 1966), OS was Behaghel (1948), for OE, Krapp and Dobbie (1931–53), and for ON, Powell (1965).

(23) Laȝ 15971

    C: Þis isah þe leodking: grimme heore lates. þa **wes he awundred:** on þissere wurlde-riche.

    O: Þis fiht isah þe king: and **awondrede him.**

    'This (fight) saw the king, their grim looks. Then he was astonished (he wondered himself) on this territory.'

(24) Laȝ 18006

    C: I þan flokke biforen: **he hafde** cnihtes wel icoren.

    O: In þan flocke bi-vore: **weren** cnihtes wel icore.

    'In the host before, he had (there were) knights well chosen.'

(25) Laȝ 18933

    C: Ah al þī iwille: **wel scal iwurðen.**

    O: Ac al þine wille: **wel þou salt habbe.**

    'But all thy will shall be well (thou shalt have).'

(26) Laȝ 28450

    C: Þa **wes hit itimed** þere: þat Merlin seide while.

    O: Þo **was i-funde** þare: þat Merlyn saide wile.

    'Then it happened (it was found) there, what Merlin often said.'

3.2. Usefulness of the periphrasis

Owing to the loss of the simple passive form, Old English used periphrastic passive, except for *hatte*. Among the copula, *(ge)weorðan* was frequently used as a passive auxiliary, but *wesan* was a good rival in this function and outlived. Both *Anglo-Saxon Chronicle* and Laȝamon's *Brut*, though the latter is based on an Anglo-French original, show a similar feature of having many ways of expressing 'who/which is/was called'. Variants include active and passive constructions as well as 'one/they call', and full of the synonymous expressions like OE *hatte, is (ge)haten, is (ge)cweden, is (ge)clepeden, is (ge)nemned*, and ME *ihote(n)*, etc.

The *man* periphrasis in the next chapter had been an alternative expression of the passive, and in the medieval period it served to enrich the text until it was replaced by *one*.

Chapter 4 *man*-periphrasis

4.1. Dictionary Data and Additional Data

The construction with the indefinite *man* appears a phenomenon contrary to the general tendency of auxiliation. It was used when the subject was not necessary to be expressed in the passive construction, especially with the verbs of killing and naming in the *Anglo-Saxon Chronicle*, e.g. *ChronA 755 mon ofslog Ēþelbald Miercna cyning* 'Æthelbald the Mercian king was killed' and *ChronA 514 þær mon nu nemneþ Cerdicesford* 'where is now called Cerdicesford'. A mixture of the passive, *man*-periphrasis and a unique remnant *hatte* is found in the following passage.

(27) ChronE (Irvine) 656.21, 35, 41
⁊ seo mynstre halgode seo ærcebiscop Deusdedit of Cantwarbyrig ... ⁊ seo biscop of Lundone þe **wæs** Wina **gehaten** ⁊ seo Myrcene biscop Ieruman **wæs gehaten** .... Ðas is se gife: fram Medeshamstede to Norðburh, ⁊ swa to ðet stede þet **man cleopeð** Folies, ⁊ swa æl se feon riht to Esendic, ⁊ fra Esendic to þet steode þe **man cleopeð** Feðermuðe, ... ⁊ fra Grætecros þurh an scyrwæter Bradanæ **hatte**,
'and Deusdedit the archbishop of Canterbury consecrated the monastery, ... and the bishop of London who was called Wine, and the bishop of the Mercians who was called Jaruman, ... This is the gift from Medeshamstede to Northborough and so to the place which people call Folies, and so all the fen straight to Asendike, and from Asendike to the place which people call Fethermude, ... and from Graetecros through a clear stream called Bradanae,'

In fact, *mon/man* occurred with many other verbs in various contexts.

(28) Beo 1175a
Me **man** sægde   þæt þa ðe for sunu wolde
hererinc habban.
'It has been said to me that you wished to have this warrior as a son.'

(29) CP(H) 24.179.16
On oðre wisan sint to manianne weras, on oðre wif. Ða weras **mon** sceal hefiglecor ⁊ stiðlecor læran, ⁊ ða wif leohtlecor;
'Men are to be admonished in one way, women in another way. Men are to be taught more seriously and severely, women more lightly.'

(30) Bo 7.19.9
Swa him **mon** mare selð, swa hine ma lyst.
'The more he is given, the more he desires.'

A use of *man*-periphrasis is followed by a passive in

(31) Or 6 34.152.22-23
Þa bæd he self þæt hiene mon ær gefulwade, ⁊ þa he gefulwad wæs, ...
'then he himself asked that he should be baptised first, and when he was baptised ...'

The choice of "indirect" expression in contrast to the active sentence continued in Ælfic's works, as in

(32) ÆCHom I, 11 266.3
Ic wolde eow trahtnian þis godspel þe man nu beforan eow rædde:
'I wished to interpret you this gospel which was now read in front of you'

(33) ÆLS (AshWed) 116
Gif man læt nu ænne þeof to slege hu wenst ðu?
'If a thief were now being led to be killed, how do you think?'

Mon/man was weakened to *me* and appeared in the *Peterborough Chronicle*, even before the famous passage in the year 1137 (i.e. *Me henged* ... 'they hung'). A distinctive use between the noun *se man* and the weakened indefinite pronoun *me* is clearly seen in (35).

(34) ChronE (Irvine) 1110.25
Ðises geare me began ærost to weorcenne on þam niwan mynstre on Ceortesæge.
'In this year people began to work first on the new monastery at Chertsey.'

(35) ChronE (Irvine) 1124.47
Ful heui gær wæs hit: se man þe æni god heafde, him me hit beræfode mid strange geoldes ⁊ mid strange motes; þe nan ne heafde stærf of hungor.
'It was a very hard year: the man who had any property was deprived of it by heavy tribute and by strong court; (he) who had none died of hunger.'

Then here is a series of *me*-periphrases, in which *hengen* and *uurythen* have plural endings, and is followed by a construction with plural 'they', i.e.

(36) ChronE (Irvine) 1137.264
Me henged up bi the fet ⁊ smoked heom mid ful smoke. Me henged bi the þumbes other bi the hefed ⁊ hengen bryniges on her fet. Me dide cnotted strenges abuton here hæued ⁊ uurythen it ðat it gæde to þe hærnes. Hi diden heom in quaterne ...
'They hung them up by the feet and smoked them with foul smoke. They hung them by the thumbs or by the head and hung coats of mail on their feet. They put knotted strings around their head and twisted it until it went into the brain. They put them into a torture box, ...'

30

In Laȝmon's *Brut* the use of *man/me* can be traceable.[1]

(37) Laȝ 25949
C: næs nan kēpen iboren: of nauer nare burden.
þat **mon** ne mæi mid strēðe: stupen hine to grunde.
O: nas neuere kempe ibore: of none brude.
þat **me** ne may mid strengþe: stoupe to grunde.
'no champion had ever been born of any lady, who can be stooped down
to the ground with strength.'

Earlier occurrences of the weakened but not shortened form *men* are attested in *MED* (**men** (pron. indef.)), which is dated *c*1150 (OE).

(38) Hrl.HApul. (Hrl 6258B) 98.62/1
Þeos wyrt, þat **men** gladiolum ..emned [read: nemneð].
TrinHom 155
Nis nefre no stede .. ne hure riht time þenne **men** fasten shal.

Also under the same headword two examples from the Wycliffite are quoted, *men* in *EV* but *me* or *thei* in *LV*; judging from the verb forms (i.e. in
the plural, not in the singular), Old English versions do not seem to use this
periphrasis in these contexts.

(39) Mt 5.15 [neque accendunt lucernam et ponunt eam sub modio]
Li: ne ec bernas ðæccille ł leht-fæt ꞇ settas ða ł hia under (*sic*) mitte ł under
sestre
Ruʹ1: ne menn blæcern in beornað ꞇ settaþ hine under mytte
WSCp: Ne hi ne ælað hyra leoht-fæt. ꞇ hit under cyfe settað.
WycEV: nether **men** tendyn a lanterne, and putten it vndir a busshel,
WycLV: ne **me** teendith not a lanterne, and puttith it vndur a busschel,
AV: Neither doe men light a candle, and put it vnder a bushell

(40) Gen (B) 11.2 [Cumque proficiscerentur de oriente, inuenerunt campum in
terra Sennaar, et habitauerunt in eo.]
Ða ða hi ferdon fram eastdæle, hi fundon ænne feld on Senaarlande, ꞇ
wunodon ðæron.

---

1   *Men*, plural of the noun *man*, appears in a sentence, which corresponds to a passive construction as a manuscript variant: Laȝ 7023 (C) *Ældolf men cleopeden
þene king*; (O) *Deldol was i-hote* 'men called the king Ældolf (he was named
Deldol)'.

WycEV: And whan men shulden go² [Bod 959: **men schulde gone**] fro the est, thei founden a feeld in the lond of Sennaer, and thei dwelleden in it.
WycLV: And whanne thei ȝeden forth fro the eest, thei fonden a feeld in the lond of Sennaar, and dwelliden ther ynne.
   AV: And it came to passe as they iourneyed from the East, that they found a plaine in the land of Shinar, and they dwelt there.

Before the establishment of *one* in the fifteenth century, we find *an/on* in Laȝamon, as in

(41) Laȝ 7043 (=3511 by *MED*)
   C: Seoððen com **an** þe leouede wel: he hæhte Famel-penicel.
   O: Suþþe com **on** þat lifde wel: þat hehte Samupensel.
   'Then came one who lived well; he (who) was called Famul-Penicel (Samupensel).'

The earliest example of the indefinite pronoun *one* can be seen in *Cursor Mundi*, as *OED3* (*one*, C. pron, VI. 17a, referred to *MED*) quotes, as in

(42) Cursor 1023
   C: Of **an** qua siþen ete at þe last, / he suld in eild be ai stedfast,
   G: Of **ane** qua-so it etes at the last, / He sal in elde be euer stedfast,
   T: Of **oon** who so eteþ at þe last / In oon elde shal he euer be fast

The next example is *a*1425 (*c*1385) Chaucer *Troilus & Criseyde* II. 892 *They weren all be love, if **oon** be hoot* is.

4.2. Usefulness of the periphrasis

Man-periphrasis was useful when a writer did not want to specify or identify a person who took part in the action, in contrast with topicalisation. Since the '*be* + past participle' construction had already established in Old English, *man*-periphrasis functioned as a stylistic variant from early Old English period. It became restricted in occurrence in late Old English but survived into Mddle English until *man/me(n)* was replacedby *one*.³

---

2   Forshall-Madden (1850) uses MS Corpus Christi College Oxford 4 for the Hexateuch.
3   For the use of *one* see Rissanen (1967).

Chapter 5   *beon/wesan* + present participle

5.1. Dictionary Data and Additional Data

In *DOE* bēon, under B.14.b.ii. rendering the Latin periphrastic future, an example is quoted from the Lindisfarne gloss: *LkGl(Li)* 7.20 *tu es qui uenturus es an alium expectamus ðu arð seðe tocymende wæs ł arð ł oðer we abidas* (ACpR *eart*, H *ert*). It should be noted that L. *uenturus esse* is almost always translated as *tocymende is/arð/wæs/wære* (not *biþ/beoþ/bist*), probably because the futurity is rendered by the set of '*beon/wesan* + present participle', not by the verb *beon* alone. Under B.14.c.i. *beon* + present participle expressing duration, we see: *LawAtEl* 4 *ara ðinum fæder & þinra medder, ða þe Dryhten seald, þæt ðu sie þy leng libbende on eorþan* (G *sie*, HLd *sy*; cf. Quadr. *ut sis longeuus sper terram*). OE *libban* is often used in the present participle to express duration, especially in Ælfric. Under B.14.c.ii. *beon* + present participle expressing habitual or recurring action, an example is given from *Orosius: Or 3* 7.65.8 *Philippuse geþuhte þa þæt he leng mid folcgefeohtum wið hie ne mehte; ac oftrædlice he wæs mid hloþum on hi hergende, & onbutan sierwende oþ hie eft totwæmde wæron*. *Orosius* prefers using the present participle in early Old English texts.

A simple verb form and a '*be* + pres ptc' may occur in the same or a similar context as variants, as in

(43)   Chron 855
   A: ⁊ þy ilcan geare ferde to Rome mid micelre weorþnesse ⁊ þær **was** XII monaþ **wuniende** ⁊ þa him hamweard for
   E: And þy ilcan geare ferde to Rome mid mycclum wurðscipe ⁊ þær **wunade** XII monað,

which means that the periphrasis may well express duration in some contexts, but simple verb forms can be used in a series of paratactic constructions.

It should also be noted that in the construction '*see/hear* + someone/something + *-ing*' was, though examples were found in Old English, the present participle originally agreed with the object (i.e. someone/something), as found in the following examples.

(44) HomS 24 (ScraggVerc 1) 69

Soð is þonne þæt ic eow secge ðæt nu hwænne <gelimpeð> þæt ge geseoð mannes sunu **sittendne** [E: **sittende**] on þa swiðran healfe Godfæder in heofonwolcnum,

'It is true then that I tell you that now it happens when you see the son of man sitting on the right-hand side of Father God in heavens'

(45) GD 2(H) 14.132.9

⁊ þa þa he feorron geseah hine **sittendne**. þa ne dorste he him to genealæcean, ac he hine sylfne on eorðan astrehte.

'and when from afar he saw him sitting, then he dared not draw near to him but stretched himself on the ground'

In both examples the form *sittendne* agrees with *sunu* and *hine*, the accusative. In the Verc Hom MS. A (x^2) *sittendne* has a variant *sittende* in MS. E (xi[in]), and GD MS. H is dated xi[1]; this means that the case agreement of the present participle was still visible in the eleventh century.

The development of *–ing* form involves morphological confusion of the inflectional endings of the present participle, the bare infinitive and the inflected infinitive, and the verbal noun. The following diagram may show the confusion in Middle English dialects.[1]

	OE	ME	
present participle	-ende	-ande	
		-ende	
			-inge
		-inde	
infinitive	-an	-(e)n, -in, -yn	
to-infinitive	-enne	-en, -in; -ing(e)	
		-enne, -ende	
verbal noun	-ung	-ing	
	-ing		

---

1   For information of morphological varieties see Baugh & Cable (1993), Campbell (1959), Mossé (1952), Moore & Knott (1975) and Moore & Marckwardt (1969).

The form *-ing(e)* appeared in Midland around the twelfth century as the inflected ending of the present participle and also of the *to*-infinitive; as the ending of a verbal noun *-ing* had been used from Old English. The endings *-ende*, *-inde* and *-inge* as variant forms are found in Laʒamon, as in:

	Calig.	Otho
1582	Ne ganninde ne ridinde	Ne goinde ne ridīgge
6433	Wnder þon hær cō tidinde	Onder þan come tidinge
7321	for þes tidende him wes læð	for þes tidinge him was loþ
7406	Sone come þa tiðende	Sone come þe tidinge
8084	ane þechene bærninde	ane tapere bernende
15561	heo bigunnen striuinge	hii bi-gonne to striuende
16579	þær þ ganninde folc	þar þat going folk
17466	Þat tidende com to þan kinge	Þe tydinge com to þan kinge
26228	an(d) hiʒende he wes ido	an hiʒeng hit was ido
26946	heo riden singinge	hii ...... singende
28524	ridinde & ganninde	ridende and . ohinge

There is an interesting example, in which a simple verb form shows a contrast with '*be + on + -ing*'; this may suggest the development of the '*be + present participle*' construction through the fusion with '*be + on + verbal noun*'.[2]

(46) Laʒ 6630
C: & heo him þene kīg tahten: þer he **hundede** [huntede?] on comelan.
O: and hii þane king tahte: war he **was an hontinge**.
'and they directed him to the king, where he hunted (was a-hunting) in a valley'

The morphological confusion between the inflectional endings of the present participle *-ende* and the inflected infinitive *-enne* posed another problem. In Ogura (2009) I summarised my survey and said that it was around the eleventh century when the confusion had started, because most of manuscripts dated back around that period. But it could be earlier, when examples of double glosses of *-enne* and *-ende* are found in the glosses of the Lindisfarne and Rushworth Gospels, in the form of alternative expressions in *Bede* and Gregory's *Dialogues*, the confusion (or the recognition

---

2   Cf. Laʒ 12326 (C) *Þus Gratien þe king for ut an slæting* [O: *vt wende an hontīge*] 'Thus Gracien the king went out a-hunting.'

of the two forms as variants) has started when Old English appeared as a written medium. Here are some examples.

(47) Jn 1.31 [sed ut manifestaretur in israhel propterea ueni ego in aqua **baptizans**]
Li: ah þte were adeaued in Israel foreðon ł æfterðon cuom ic in uætre fulguande ł to ful*guanne*
Ru2: ah þte were æt-eowed folche isr*a*el forðon ł æfter ðæm ic com ic in wætre **gifulwad wæs**
WSCp: ac ic cóm ⁊ **fullode** on wǽtere to ðæm þ he wære geswutelud on israhela folce.
WycEV: but that he be schewid in Israel, therfore I cam **baptisinge** in watir.
AV: but that he should be made manifest to Israel, therefore am I come **baptizing** with water

(48) Jn 7.25 [none hic est quem quer*unt* **interficere**]
Li: ahne ðes is ðone soecað **to a-cuellanne**
Ru2: ah ne ðis is ðone ge-soecað **to acwellanne**
WSCp: hu nis ðis se ðe hi sceeaþ **to ofsleande**
WSA: hu nys þys se þe hig secað **to ofsleanne**
WycEV: Wher this is not, whom the Jewis seken **to slee?**
AV: Is not this hee, whome they seeke **to kill?**

These two examples from *Jn* show the literary translation of *Li*, and (47) the free translations in *Ru2* and *WSCp*, while (48) illustrates the different choice between *-ende* and *-enne* in *WSCp* and *WSA* after the preposition *to*. This is not the only example where *WSCp* uses *to -ende* instead of *to -enne*, which may suggest that the use of *to*, as well as the similar place of articulation between [d] and [n], could be a cause of the fusion of the two endings. Manuscript variants are found in other texts than the Gospels, some of which I quote here (for more examples and details see Ogura (2009)).

(49) Bede 2.2 100.29
þonne ís he gelyfed þæt he Cristes geoc bere ⁊ eow lære **to beorenne** [T: beor-renne (beor *ends* 6ᵇ, renne *begins* 7ᵃ), O: beranne, Ca: berenne, B: berende] 'then it is credible that he should bear the yoke of Christ and teach you to bear it'

(50) HomS 40.1 (Nap49) 253.4-13 (cf. HomS 40.3 (ScraggeVerc10) 198.45-52)
ne syn we to gifre ne to frece ne to firenlustgeorne ne to æfestige ne to inwit-fulle ne to tælende ne to twigspræce ne morðor to begangenne [D: to frem-menne] ne aðas **to swerjanne** [D: to swerigende, K: to swerianne] ne niðas to fremmanne [D: to hæbbenne] ne leasunga to secganne [D: to secgenne] ne þeofênde to begangenne; ne werignessa we ne **fyljan** [D: to fyligende, K: to fyligenne] ne heafodlice leahtras ne lufjan ne scyncræftas onhyrgen ne

galdorsangas ne unriht lyblac onginnen ne to ýdbelige ne syn ne to langsum yrre hæbben, ne in oferhydo we ne scylon gewitan.

'Nor let us be too greedy, nor too rash, nor too wanton, nor too envious, nor too wicked, nor too slanderous, nor too deceitful [*lit.* double-tongued], neither for to commit murder, nor for to speak lies, nor for to engage in thefts, nor let us practice abuse, nor let us love the deadly sins, nor let us extol either sorceries or incantations, nor let us undertake wicked witchcraft; nor let us be too easily irritated [nor] having too lasting anger.' (tr. by K. J. MacArthur)

(51) Ps 118.62 [Media nocte surgebam **ad confitendum** tibi super iudicia iustitiae tuae][3]

    A: on midde naeht ic aras **to ondetende** ðe ofer domas rehtwisnisse ðinre
    B: to midre niht ic aras **to ondettenne** de ofer domas dinre ryhtwisnesse
    D: on midre nihte ic aras **to andettenne** ðe ofer domas rihtwisnesse þinre
    I: on middre nihte ic aras **to andettenne** ðe ofer domas rihtwisnesse þinre
WycEV: At myd nyȝt I ros **to knouleche** to thee; vp on the domes of thi iustefiyng.
    AV: At mid-night I will rise **to giue thankes** vnto thee: because of thy righteous iudgements.
    Cf.   HomS 11.2 (ScraggVerc3) 36.68 [Media nocte surgebam ad confitendum tibi super iudicia iustificationis (*v.l.* iustitiae) tuae] To middere nihte ic wæs arisende þe **to andettanne** ofer þa domas þinre rihtwisnesse. 'At midnight I rose up to praise thee over thy righteous judgement.'

(52) Chron 604
    A (604.3):   Mellitum he sende **to bodiende** <Eastseaxum> fulluht,
    E (604.3):   Mellitum he sende **to bodianne** Eastseaxum fulluht,
               'he sent Mellitus to preach Christianity to the East Saxons'

(53) Chron 1048 & 1050
    F (1050.16):   ac se eorl nolde geþwærian farðan him was lað **to amyrrende** his agen.
    E (1048.36):   ⁊ se eorl nolde na geðwærian þære infare, forþan him wæs lað **to amyrrene** his agenne folgað.
               'and the earl would not agree to the invasion, because it was loathsome for him to injure the people of his own district'

Example (51) from the Psalter gives us an idea that the Latin infinitive, present participle, and '*ad* + accusative of gerund' had a chance to be rendered into OE '*to* + *-enne*' and '*to* + *-ende*' constructions.

---

3   For the relation between these psalter glosses see Kitson (2002, 2003) and Ogura (2003b, 2004b, 2005b).

To -ende/-enne variants are often found in Laȝamon; MS. *C* has *–e(n)* or *-enne*, while MS. *O* shows *-ende*.

	Calig.	Otho
1156	of þa kingen[4] þa werē to kumen	þat weren to cumende
1570	Þe king sette to fleonne	Þe kinge sette to flende
4662	and Brennes to flenne	and Brennes gon to fleonde
6407	he turnde to fleme	he tornde to flende
6808	Elidur to flænne	Elidur to flende
14714	& Henḡ gon to flonnen	And Hengest gan to flende
21266	& gon him to charren	and gan him to flende
21735	and gunnen to fleonnen	and gonne to fleonde
23989	and leoden to fleonen	and þat oþer folk to fleonde
27215	and biginnen to fleō	and sette to fleonde
30653	þat him weoren to cumēe	þat him to coming were
Cf. 11365	sette to fleonde	sette to flende

The construction '*be* + present participle' took quite a long time to be established in the English tense system owing to these complicated morphological and syntactic circumstances.

5.2. Usefulness of the periphrasis

The "durative colour" and "descriptive force", which were brought forth by using this periphrasis, were already maintained by Mustanoja (1960: 584–5). Lanout (2015) examines this periphrasis as a stylistic tool, which seems a good viewpoint, although it is hard to prove it in an obvious way. Mustanoja's "descriptiveness" was probably the first stage of the use of this periphrasis, since the present participle was regarded as an adjective, and then '*be* + pres ptc' began to establish itself in the tense system. Even in Old English we find verbs of fighting and living often chose this syntactic exnvironment.[5] To examine the history of the development of this periphrasis is meaningful, or rather, to examine which verb was more frequently used in this periphrasis is still more important.

---

4   Read *þingen*.
5   For a detailed study on verbs see Ogura (2014).

Chapter 6 *onginnan/beginnan* + infinitive

6.1. Dictionary Data and Additional Data

According to *OED3* **begin**, *v.*[1], 1. intr. a., two earlier quotations are notice-able: *c*1000 Ælfric *Genesis* ix.20 *Noe þa began to wircenne þæt land* and *c*1175 *Lamb. Hom.* 77 *Nu bi-gon paul to wepan.* Mutanoja (1960: 611) states that "OE *onginnan*, when it occurs as an auxiliary with an infinitive, can be said to carry out two principal functions: (1) it brings out the ingres-sive and perfective aspects of the action represented by the infinitive, and (2) it intensifies the descriptive force of infinitive." Mitchell (*OES*, § 676) wonders if the same verb may have the ingressive and perfective aspects and in the next section (§ 677) quotes the following examples:

(54) Dream 27a
Ongan þa word sprecan   wudu selesta:
'Then the best of woods started to speak words:'

(55) Dream 73b
        Þa us man fyllan **ongan**
ealle to eorðan.   Þæt wæs egeslic wyrd!
'Then we were all felled to the ground. That was a fearful fate!'

(56) GenA 2717a
        Þa **ongan** Abimæleh   Abraham swiðan
woruldgestreonum   and him his wif ageaf.
'Then Abimelech endowed Abraham with treasure, and gave him his wife again.'

(57) Beo 244b
No her cuðlicor   cuman **ongunnon**
lindhæbbende;
'No shield-bearers have ever arrived here more openly' (translation mine)
'No strangers have ever begun to land here more openly with their shields' (by Clark Hall and Wrenn (1940))

Example (54) seems a general use of *onginnan* in the sense of 'to begin', while (55) is one of the examples quoted by Terasawa (1974) to show the feature of *onginnan* similar to ME *gan*, (56) by Mustanoja (1960) similar to periphrastic *do*, in contrast with (57) by Wrenn who translates as the perfect. The meaning of *ongan* tends to vary, especially the verb appears in

39

a *b*-verse and the infinitive occupies the alliterating position. Though Mitchell says that this is a "very subjective question" (§ 677), this means that OE *onginnan* had already shown a functional fracture and a threshold of grammaticalisation. I revise the diagram in Ogura (1997b: 404) as follows:

	OE	ME
'to begin'	onginnan	
	aginnan	aginnen
	beginnan	beginnen
	ginnaan	ginnen
'to attack'	onginnan	
	beginnan	
'to undertake'	onginan	beginnen
	aginnan	ginnen
as an auxiliary	onginnan	ginnen
	beginnan	beginnen

As a preterite auxiliary *onginnan* and *ginnan* had been in use, which was involved into a dialectal variation of *con* and *gan* in Middle English, while *onginnan* and *beginnan* were also used in inceptive mood, and developed into the *begin to* construction. The morphological fusion and the subsequent separation between *began* and *gan* (i.e. especially in the preterite forms) could be illustrated as follows.[1]

ongan → angan → agan → gan/con   [preterite auxiliary]
                         did, (gert)
began ----------------------→ began   [ingressive aspect]

DOE gives only two examples of OE *ginnan*, one from *Bede* and the other from a gloss for *initia*; the former is given here.[2]

---

1 See Ogura (1997b: 425).
2 See *DOE* **ginnan** Vb. st. 3.

(58) Bede 1 15.60.22 [At ubi datam sibi mansionem intrauerant, coeperunt ap-
ostolicam primitiuae ecclesiae uitam imitari]
Ða wæs sona ðæs þe heo inneodon in þa eardugstowe þe him alyfed wæs
in þære cynelecan byrig, ða **gunnon** [B & Ca: **ongunon**; O: **ongunnan**] heo
þæt apostolice lif þære frymðelecan cyrcan onhyrgan
'Soon after that they (Augustine and his companions) entered the dwelling-
place, which was allotted to them in the royal city, then they began to imitate
the apostolical life of the primitive church'

This construction often takes an infinitive, but sometimes an inflected infinitive appears: *ÆCHomI, 11* 268.62 *Her began se deoful to reccenne
halige gewritu* 'Here the devil began to interpret the Holy Writ' (see *DOE*
be-ginnan). Four early Middle English examples can be quoted to show
morphological fusion in the development of this periphrasis. (Examples
from *Orm* are originally in *MED*, but I expand a little.)

(59) Orm 2801–2, 2805, 2808, 2809–10
Min child i blisse sone **onngann**
   To blissenn i min wambe,
Þatt wass swa summ ȝho seȝȝde þuss
   Wiþþ opennlike spæche,
Son sum þu **gann to gretenn** me
   Wiþþ þine milde wordess,
Min child tatt i min wambe liþ
   Bigann itt te **to þannkenn**,
Forr he **bigann** forrþrihht anan
   To stirenn ⁊ to buttenn;
'My child soon began to rejoice in my womb in bliss, that was just as she said
thus with plain speech, soon you began to greet me with your mild words,
my child who lies in my womb began to thank you for it, for he began im-
mediately to move and to push.'

(60) Orm 3274, 3276
⁊ he wass wurrþenn Kaserrking
   Off all mannkinn onn eorþe,
⁊ he **gann þennkenn** off himm sellf.
   ⁊ off hiss miccle riche.
⁊ he **bigann to þennkenn** þa,
   Swa sum þe Goddspell kiþeþþ,[3]

---

3 Infinitives were used with or without *to* in the transitional period, when inflectional endings became ambiguous. Cf. Laȝ 23611 (C) *For leouere me is to liggen*,
(O) *For leuere me his ligge.*

'and he had become Emperor of all mankind on earth, and he began to think of himself and of his great kingdom, and he began to consider them, just as the Gospel tells'

(61) Laȝ 8144
C: Þeos tweien cnihtes **bi-gunnen:** mid sceldes **to scurmen.**
O: Þeos twei cnihtes **bi-gonnen:** **to sceremigge.**
'These two knights began to skirmish with shields.'

(62) Laȝ 15561
C: Vmbē ane stunde: heo **bigunnen striuinge.**
O: Bi one lutele stunde: hii **bi-gonne to striuende.**
'After a little while they began striving (to strive)'

A similar expression, which I mentioned in Ogura (1997b: 423–5), had been found in a very limited period and in very limited texts with a Northern feature, that is, eME '*taken to* + infinitive' (see *OED3* **taken** v. 55. †a. and *MED* **taken** 37a.).

(63) ChronE (Irvine) 1135.19
⁊ Dauid king of Scotland **toc to uuerrien** him;
'and David king of Scotland, began to make war upon him'

(64) Orm 4772–3, 4780–4
Swa swiþe þatt hiss bodiȝ **toc**
To rotenn bufenn eorþe
┊
⁊ all he **toc** forrþrihht anan
To rŏtenn ⁊ to stinnkenn
⁊ war ⁊ wirrsenn **toc** anan
Ȗt off hiss lic **to flowenn.**
'So great that his body began to decay above the earth … he straightway began to decay completely and to stink, and humour and corruption soon began to flow out of his body.'

(65) Orm 2203
He **toc to frofrenn** hire anann
Cuþliȝ bi name, ⁊ seȝȝde;
Ne beo þu, Marȝe, nohht forrdredd,
Þin Godd art tu full deore.
'He began to comfort her continuously, openly by name, and said, Mary, do not be afraid, you are very dear to your God.'

(66) Cursor (C) 12029
þan **tok** ioseph ie*sus* **to ledde** / Maria and þai ham-ward yede;

As I mentioned earlier, *ChronE*, *Orm* and *Cursor (C)* are all texts with a Northern feature, but in *MED* we find an example from Bodley 34, West Midland: *c1225(?1200) St.Kath(1)* (Bod34) 108/752 *Sone se ha þis sehen .. alle somet turnden, ant token to ʒeien, 'Witherliche, muche wurð and wurðe alle wurðschipe is þes meidenes go[d]d Crist … .*

6.2. Usefulness of the periphrasis

Not only the development of the ingressive aspect but the intertwined development of this periphrasis, the *gan/con* periphrasis, periphrastic *do* and causative auxiliaries is the key to make medieval syntax manifest. These phenomena cross the morphological, syntactic and semantic fields so freely that my chapters 6, 7, 8 and 10 co-relate inseparably. From late Old English to early Middle English, owing to both linguistic and non-linguistic causes, the language was forced to be more periphrastic to convey subtle shades of meaning which came out by internal and external forces – internal as the morphological ambiguity that started from the levelling of case endings, and external as Old Norse and Anglo-Norman French influences before their great debut in medieval texts from the thirteenth century onwards. These periphrases should not be considered separately, because they had been connected closely and complicatedly in the process of their development.

Chapter 7 *gan/con* + infinitive

7.1. Dictionary Data and Additional Data

When we see the explanations of *OED3*, under the heading **gin**, *v.*[1] *Obs. exc. arch.* 1. a. *intr.*: "To begin, followed by inf. active, with or without *to*; rarely *for to*. In Middle English poetry the pa.t. *gan* was commonly used in a weakened sense, as a mere auxiliary (= the modern *did*) serving to form a periphrastic preterite; the altered form CAN *v.*[2] became, however, more frequent in this use." The first and second examples are: *a*1200 *Moral Ode* 272 *Þo þe .. gunnen here gultes beter and betere lif leden*, and ?*c*1200 *Ormulum* (Burchfield transcript) l. 3274 *He gann þennkenn off himm sellf.* As to the verb **can** *v.*[2] Chiefly *Sc.* in later use *Obs.*, three syntactic environments are explained under I. In form *can* (or *con*, etc.): "1. Followed by bare infinitive, as a periphrastic auxiliary of the past tense, a. With infinitive of a main verb, e.g. *tho can she weepe* 'then she wept'; = *did* (see DO *v.* 32a (a)); 2. Followed by *to*-infinitive. Began, proceeded *to* do something; = *gan* (see GIN *v*[1].). Much less usual than *gan* in this sense; 3. Followed by bare infinitive, as a periphrastic auxiliary of the present tense, e.g. *þon conez saye* 'you say'; = *do* (see DO *v.* 32a (a)). Only attested in *Pearl*." The last statement suggests that the use of *can/con* as a present preterite auxiliary may be restricted to this particular poem of North-West Midland in MS Cotton Nero A.x (*Pearl* 482 ȝ*yf hyt be soth þat þou conez saye* and 1077 [1078] *Þat twelue fryteȝ of lyf con bere ful sone*). *MED* **can** (v.) (b) has another example: *Pearl* 294 *Þy worde byfore þy wytte con fle*, and actually the first example under (b) is ?*a*1300 *Thrush & N.* (Dgb 86) 33 *Hy gladieþ .. Boþe þe heye and þe lowe; Mid gome hy cunne hem grete.* The present auxiliary *con* could be a feature of West Midland, but it would be safe to say that it started in the late thirteen centry South-West Midland.

Variant forms of '*gan* + infinitive', '*gan* + *to*-infinitive', and a simple verb, can be found in Laȝamon, as in:[1]

---

1   Cf. Examples of the manuscript variants of Laȝamon in Chapter 5.

	Calig.	Otho
14072	& fæire hine gon greten	and faire hine grette
15396–7	& him seolf Vortiger neʒ	And Vortiger gan wendeʒ
	flæh ouer Sæuærne.	ouer Séévarne.
17116	he hine fræinien gon	and he axede him anon
19868	Vðer þe græten	Þe king þe gan grete
22421	& he gon andswerie	and him andswerede
23717	and he lehʒen agon	Arthur gan to lahʒe
23756	duʒeðe gunne sturien	þat folk gā to storie
25987	and þa six swin he gon æten alle	and alle þe six swyn he eat
27745	& bi-halues him eode	and he bi-halues gan gon
Cf. 4662	and Brennes to flenne	and Brennes gon to fleonde
17351	gon him to fleonne þar	gan to fleonde þar

These examples show that a simple verb and a periphrasis are variants to be used in late thirteenth century South-West Midland. Moreover, it seems not always true that *gan* appears in the South and East Midland and *con* in the North and West Midland, as shown in the diagrams in Chapter 10. One example from Laʒamon can be quoted here.

(67) Laʒ 23205
C: And Riculf him **gon rideʒ** to-ʒæines Arður anan.
O: And Riculf **cō rideʒ** to-ʒeines Arthure a-non.
'and Riculf rode against Arthur immediately'

Variants are found in the four manuscripts of *Cursor Mundi*, where the infinitives (with or without *to*) are set at the end of the line for the endrhyme owing to the use of periphrastic *gan/con/dud*.[2] MS. *F* often follows MS. *C*, though not always.

(68) Cursor 758
C: þe nedder nerhand hir **gun draw**
G: þe nedd*er* nere hand hir **gan drau**
F: þe nedder nerhande hir **con ga**
T: þe nedder neʒe to hir **gon drawe**

(69) Cursor 838
C: þar þai biginning **gan to tak**
G: þair biginning **gan** þai at hi*m* take
F: þer þai **con** be-gynnyng*e* take
T: þe*re* bigynnynge **dud** þei take

---

2   Cf. Examples of the manuscript variants of *Cursor Mundi* in Chapter 10.

(70) Cursor 2008–9

    C: **Bigan** neu biginyng **for to dight**, A neu liuelade **cun** þai **bigin**

    G: A neu biginning **gan** he **dight**, A neu liuelad **gan** he **bigin**

    F: **bi-gan** new þingis **to diȝt**. a new liuelade þai **con be-gyn**

    T: A newe liflode he **dud bigynne** To newe liflode went þe be

(71) Cursor 3016

    C: Gret ioi **can** his frendes **mak**

    G: Gret ioy **gan** his freindis **mak**

    F: grete ioy **con** his frendis **make**

    T: Greet ioye **dud** his frendes **make**

(72) Cursor 13557

    C: Fast þai **can** on him **to stare**

    G: Fast þai **gan** on him **stare**

    F: fast þai **con** on him **stare**

    T: Fast **gon** þai on him **stare**

We may find more examples of manuscript variants in other texts in *MED* under can (v.): *c*1325 *Horn* (Hrl 2253) 187 *Payenes þer connen [Cmb: gunne] aryue*, *c*1390 *PPl.A(1)* (Vrn) 9.109 *And er we weoren war, with Wit cone [B,C: gan] we meeten*, etc.

7.2. Usefulness of the periphrasis

This periphrasis has a close connection with the development of the periphrastic *do* and causative auxiliaries in Middle English. The dialectal choice of *con/can* (North and West) and *gan/gon* (South and East) is mostly correct, although some manuscripts follow the choice of the preceding texts without reconsideration. It was useful to put *con/gan* immediately after the subject and put the infinitive at the end of the verse line for end-rhyme, and the device was accepted during the Middle English period. After they were ousted by *do/did*, the periphrasis itself became obsolete.

Chapter 8 *don* periphrasis

8.1. Dictionary Data and Additional Data

Engblom (1938), Ellegård (1953), Mustanoja (1960) and Visser (1963–73) are the first sources to be refrerred to, as well as *OED3*, *MED* and *DOE*. In contrast with the vicarious or pro-verbal *do* proposed by Sweet as an origin of the periphrastic *do*, most scholars now accept the causative *do* by Ellegård. When the weakening of the causative sense is considered, the use of *gan/con* as a preterite auxiliary in the Middle English period should be explained first. *MED* **ginnen** (v.) 3b has the following explanation.

> As a weak auxiliary used with infinitives to form phrases denoting actions or events as occurring (rather than as beginning to occur): do, did: (a) with past meaning; **gan eten**, did eat, ate, etc.; (b) with present or future meaning; **ginneth maken**, doth make, makes, etc. [Cp. the weak auxiliary **can**, a blend which has forms of **connen**, senses of **ginnen**; also the weak auxiliary uses of **aginnen**, **beginnen** 6., **comsen**, **connen** 2. (c), **don** 11b.]

Earlier examples of *ginnen* given there are: (a) *c*1275 (?*a*1200) Lay. *Brut* (Clg A.9) 25987 *Þa six swin he gon æten* [Otho: *he eat*] *alle ær he arise of selde*, and (b) *a*1250 (?*c*1150) Prov. *Alf.* (*Glb A. 19-James) 100/265 *Ne ȝin þe* [Jes-O: *schaltu*] *nefre þi wif bi hire wlite chesen*. The forms of *can* are found in: *c*1250 *Wolle ye i-heren* (Trin-C B.14.39) 52 *þe sterre was boþen sotel & sene; into bedlehem heo hem con lede*, and *c*1325 *Horn* (Hrl 2253) 187 *Payenes þer connen* [Cmb: *gunne*] *aryue*. The earliest example of *comsen*, a loan verb which develops into MnE *commence*, as an auxiliary (as a main verb it is used already in *c*1225 St Juliana) is: *c*1330 *Le Freine* (Auch) 270 *He gan deuise .. her gentrise ..& comced to loue hir anon riȝt*. *Aginnen*, a weakened form of OE *onginnan* shows an example earlier than other verbs naturally: *c*1150 (?OE) *PDidax* (Hrl 6258b) 49/24 *He agynþ to brecanne, þane to spiwanne*.

MED explains the periphrastic use of *do* under *don* (v.) 11b: "Unstressed **don** plus inf., used as the equivalent of the simple verb [hard to distinguish from the emphatic **do** phrase, occasionally even from the causal **do** phrase]", and quotes an example from *Horn*, which is also quoted as the

49

first example in *OED3*: *c*1300 (?1225) *Horn* (Cmb Gg.4.27) 930 *A writ he dude deuise, Aþulf hit dude write.*

In *OED3* **do**, *v*., under II. As an auxiliary verb, *Causative uses, Old English examples of both glosses and prose texts are shown †(a) With bare infinitive: eOE (Mercian) *Vespasian Psalter* 38.11 *Tabescere fecisti .. animam eius: aswindan ðu des .. sawle his*, OE *Paris Psalter* 103.30 *He .. deð hi for his egsan ealle beofian*, ?*a*1160 *Anglo-Saxon Chron.* 1140 *Þe biscop of Wincestre .. dide [heom] cumen þider*, (b) With *to*-infinitive, now *arch.* and *rare*: eOE CP 46.357 *Swa hwa swa urum wordum & gewritum hieran nylle, do hit mon us to witanne.* Under ***As periphrastic auxiliary with main verbs, a good, very long but appropriate explanation is now found, which I should like to represent here.

> 31. *trans.* As periphrastic auxiliary in imperatives.
>> OE Jn(WSCp) 8.11 Do ga [Li geong l gaea, Ru gaa, WSH: do ga; L. *vade*] & ne synga þu næfre ma.
>> OE Paris Psalter 118.25 Do me æfter þisum wordum wel gecwician [L. *vivifica me*].
>> *c*1225 (?*c* 1200) St. Juliana (Bodl.) 345 Do swiðe sei me.
> 32. *trans.* As periphrastic auxiliary in past and present tenses.
>> This construction appears to arise in the 13th cent. (no certain examples occur in Old English) and becomes especially frequent after 1500, first as a simple periphrastic form without perceptible difference of sense (in which use in south-western English regional dialect it practically takes the place of the simple form of the verb). In standard English from the early 17th cent. onwards it becomes restricted to contexts where it is functionally parallel to other auxiliaries (perfect, progressive, and modal). Then simple affirmative with inversion of word order after certain adverbs: 'So quietly did he come that ..' (like 'So quietly has he come'). Emphatic: 'He *did* drink', 'and drink he *did*' (like 'I *will* go', 'and go I *will*'). Interrogative: 'Do you hear?' (like 'Will you hear?'). Negative: 'They do not speak' (like 'They will not speak', 'They have not spoken').
>> *do* occasionally occurs in anticipative use with a main verb in the same tense and person in Old and Middle English (cf. also sense 31a).
>> OE Ælfric *Catholic Homilies: 1st Ser.* (Royal) (1997) x.260 *Se mona deð ægðer ge wyxð ge wanað.*
>> *c*1275 (?*a*1200) Laȝamon *Brut* (Calig.) (1963) l. 4680 *Aras þer þe to-nome. swa doð [c1300 Otho doh] a feole wise tonome ariseð.*
> a. In affirmative declarative sentence, and equivalent to the simple tense.
> (a) As an auxiliary to a main verb in the infinitive.
>> Fairly frequent in Middle English, relatively frequent in early modern English (though found in only a small proportion of affirmative declarative sentences),

dying out in normal prose in the 18th cent. (perhaps in parallel with the spread of the progressive construction), but retained as a metrical resource in verse. The following Old English quotations have been proposed as examples of this construction but almost certainly show *do* in anticipative use with finite forms of the verb (respectively plural past indicative *-on* and plural present subjunctive *-en*) spelt with *-an*:

> eOE tr. Orosius *Hist.* (BL. Add.) (1980) I.x.30 *Æfter ðæm hie dydon ægþer ge cyninga ricu settan ge niwu ceastra timbredon.*
> OE Wulfstan *Canons of Edgar* (Corpus Cambr.) (1972) lv. 12 *We lærað þæt preostas swa dælan folces ælmessan þæt hig ægðer don ge God gegladian ge folc to ælmessan.*

In *DOE* **don** we find examples *Jn(WSCp)* 8.11 and *PPs* 118.25 under II.B.2. imperative (or jussive) uses, while *ÆCHom I, 10 260.52, Or 1 10.30.28, WCan 1.1.1 55* and *Bo 6.14.17* under II.B.1.a. anticipatory uses. The very long explanations in *OED3* are useful for persons (like me[1]) who regard an anticipatory use of *do* as a possible origin of the periphrastic *do*. In a causative use OE *don* is used in the imperative in *CP*, and OE *gedon* is found in *GenB* in '*uton* + infinitive' construction.

(73) CP(H) 46.357.5
Swa hwa swa urum wordum & gewritum hieran nylle, **do** hit mon us to witanne,
'If anyone will not listen to our words and letters, let it be made known to us'

(74) GenB 404b
Uton oðwendan hit nu monna bearnum,
þæt heofonrice, nu we hit habban ne moton, **gedon** þæt hie his hyldo forlæten,
þæt hie þæt onwendon þæt he mid his worde bebead.
'Let us now take it, the heavenly kingdom, away from the sons of men, now that we are not allowed to have it, let us cause that they give up His favour, so that they may change what He commanded with His words.'

The two types of the anticipatory *do* should be summed up here. First, *don* appeared preceding the main verb, in the same form of the main verb as imperative (75), present (76) and preterite (77).

(75) Jn(WSCp) 8.11
Do ga ⁊ ne synga þu næfre ma.
'Go, and sin no more.'

---

1   See Ogura (2003d), and also (2003a).

(76) CP 48.375.8

Ac ðonne we doð ægðer, ge we ða wætru **todælað** æfter kyninga herestræ-tum, ge eac us selfe habbað,

'But then we do both; we disperse the waters along the king's highways, and also have them for ourselves'

(77) Or 6 34.153.4

Þa <oferhogode> he þæt he him aðer **dyde**, oþþe **wiernde**, oþþe tigþade, ac hie let sittan þær þær hie woldon.

'Then he disdained that he did either, either refused or granted, but let them sit wherever they wanted.'

Then appeared '*don* + infinitve', as in

(78) Bo 6.14.17 [Nubibus atris condita nullum fundere possunt sidera lumen]

Swa **doð** nu ða þeostro þinre gedrefednesse **wiðstandan** minum leohtum larum.

'So does now the darkness of thy trouble resist my bright teachings.'

Cf. Met 5.21 swa nu þa þiostro þinre heortan willað minre leohtan lare wiðs-tondan

(79) WCan 1.1.1 (Fowler) 55

And we lærað þæt preostas swa dælan folces ælmessan þæt hig ægðer **don** ge God **gegladian** ge folc to ælmessan **gewænian**.

'And we teach that priests should distribute alms to people so that they do both, to please God and to accustom people to alms.'

The second type is, as it were, more grammaticalised in the way that *don* became functional and the main verb more meaningful, but it is true that both types were attested in the Old English period.

The developing use of *do* can be traced with the negative and the question. *Matthew* gives us good examples of question (*Mt* 9.28), negative imperative (*Mt* 7.6), negative question (*Mt* 13.27) and negative wh-question (*Mt* 9.14); as seen in the later two constructions, *AV* uses *do*.

(80) Mt 9.28 [creditis quia possum hoc facere uobis]

Li: gelefes ge forðon ic mæg ðis gedoa ł gewyrce iuh
Ru1: gelefaþ git þe ic mæge þæt gedoa inc
WSCp: gelýfe gyt. þ ic inc mæg gehælan.
WycEV: Bileeue ʒe, that I may do this thing to ʒou?
AV: Beleeue ye that I am able to doe this?
RSV: **Do** you believe that I am able to do this?

(81) Mt 7.6 [Nolite dare s*anctu*m canibus neq*ue* mittatis margaritas uestras ante porcos]

    Li: nellas ge sella halig hundu*m* ne sendas ge meregrotta² iurre bef*ore* berg

    Ru1: ne sellað ge halig hundum ne gewearpaþ ercnan-stanas eowre beforan swinum

    WSCp: Nellen ge syllan þ halige hundu*m*. ne ge ne wurpen eowre meregrotu toforan eowru*m* swynon.

    WycEV: Nyl ȝe ȝeue holy thing to houndis, nether sende ȝe ȝour margaritis, *or preciouse stoonys*, before swine,

    AV: Giue not that which is holy vnto the dogs, neither cast your pearles before swine:

    RSV: **Do** not give dogs what is holy; and **do** not throw your pearls before swine,

(82) Mt 13.27 [d*omi*ne nonne bonum semen seminasti in agro tuo unde ergo habet zizania]

    Li: drihten ahne god séd ðu geseawu in lónd ðinu*m* huona forðon hafes un-wæstm ɫ átih ɫ wynnung ɫ wilde foter

    Ru1: drihten no þu god sed geseowe on lond þin hwonan þonne hæfð hit þæt weod

    WSCp: hlaford hú ne seow þu god sæd on þinu*m* æcere. hwanon hæfde he coccel

    WycEV: Lord, wher thou hast nat sowen good seed in thi feeld? wher of than hath it dernel, *or cokil*?

    WycLV: Lord, whether hast thou not sowun good seed in thi feeld? where of thanne hath it taris?

    AV: Sir, **didst** not thou sow good seede in thy field? from whence then hath it tares?

    RSV: Sir, **did** you not sow good seed in your field? How then has it weeds?

(83) Mt 9.14 [quare nos et pharisaei ieiunamus frequenter discipuli autem tui non ieiunant]

    Li: forhuon woe ɫ usih ⁊ we fæstas oft ɫ symle ðegnas uutedlice ðin*n*e ne fæstas

    Ru1: for hwon we ⁊ farisei fæstaþ gelóme leorneras þonne þine ne fæstaþ

    WSCp: Hwi fæste we ⁊ þa sundor-halgan gelomlice; Soþlice þine learning-cnihtas ne fæstað.

    WycEV: Whi we and Pharisees fasten ofte, but thi disciplis fasten nat?

    AV: Why **doe** we and the Pharisees fast oft, but thy disciples fast not?

    RSV: Why **do** we and the Pharisees fast, but your disciples **do** not fast?

---

2 A long additional gloss can be seen after this word in the margin, which reads: *precepta euangelii þ aron þa meregrotta þ sindon godspelles bebodo. ante porcos before bergum ðæt sindon ða mæstelbergas þ aron ða gehadade menn and ða gode menn and ða wlonce men forhogas godes bebod ⁊ godspelles.*

8.2. Usefulness of the periphrasis

As is examined and illustrated by Ellegård (1953: 162), the periphrastic use of *do* developed from the fifteenth to the seventeenth century and spread rather slowly. The process of its general use has not been completely clarified yet, but when the Old English examples of anticipatory use is considered, the later development of periphrastic *do* in the early Modern English period should be reconsidered in relation to causative auxiliaries and preterite auxiliaries from syntactic and stylistic viewpoints (i.e. the establishment of the modern word order and the poetic use of end-rhyme). Social factors, discussed by Nurmi (1999), should also be taken into account.

Chapter 9 *uton* + infinitive

9.1. Dictionary Data and Additional Data

This is a West Saxon feature of hortative construction, an alternative to the first person plural imperative construction, and is also found mostly in prose. The VS order is not always the rule, which is very confusing outside the gloss, where the order itself cannot tell if the structure means a hortative expression or just a statement. When the translations of the Psalms are compared dialectally and diachronically, *utan/uton* appears only in (both early and late) West Saxon glosses as well as the subjunctive forms with or without inversion, while in the Wycliffite subjunctive forms and VS order appear again.

(84) Ps 94.1 [Uenite exultemus domino. iubilemuus deo salutari nostro]
- A: cumað gefen we dryhī wynsumie we gode ðæm halwyndan urum
- D: cumað **uton** blissian drihtne **uton** dryman ʒode hælende uru*m*
- I: cumaþ **utan** blissian drihtne **utan** tægnian gode urum halwendan
- WycEV: Cometh, ful out ioʒe wee to the Lord; inwardli ioʒe wee to God, our helthe ʒiuere.
- WycLV: Come ʒe, make we ful out ioie to the Lord; hertli synge we to God, oure heelthe.
- AV: Come, let vs sing vnto the Lord: let vs make a ioyfull noise to the rocke of our saluation.

(85) Ps 94.2 [Preoccupemus faciem eius in confessione et in psalmis iubilemus ei]
- A: abisgien we onsiene his in ondetnisse ⁊ in salmum wynsumie we him
- D: we ofðriccen ansiene his on andetnesse ⁊ on sealmu*m* we drymen hi*m*
- I: **utan** forhradian his ansyne on andetnesse ⁊ on sealmsangum **utan** fægnian him
- WycEV: Befor ocupie wee his face in knouleching; and in salmys inwardli ioʒe wee to hym.
- WycLV: Bifore ocupie we his face in knowleching; and hertli synge we to him in salmes.
- AV: Let vs come before his presence with thanksgiuing: and make a ioyfull noise vnto him with psalms.

(86) Ps 94.6 [Uenite adoremus et procidamus ante deum. ploremus corum domino qui fecit nos]

    A: cumað weorðien we ⁊ forðluten we biforan god woepen we biforan dryhtne se dyde usic

    D: cumað **uton** ȝebiddan ⁊ **uton** aþenian beforon ȝod we wepen beforon drihtne þe worhte

    I: **utan** gebiddan ⁊ **utan** niþerfeallen ⁊ **utan** wepan ætforan se þe geweorhte us

WycEV: Cometh, honoure wee, and falle wee doun before God, wepe wee befor the Lord, for he made vs

WycLV: Come ȝe, herie we, and falle we doun bifore God, wepe we bifore the Lord that made vs

    AV: O come, let vs worship and bowe downe: let vs kneele before the Lord our maker.

A construction combined with *don*, which is particularly found in Wulfstan, is attested and quoted in *DOE* under **don**, II.B.2.d.,[1] e.g.

(87) HomU 26 73

nu, leofan menn, **uton don**, swa man us bit and lærð, geþencan, hu feallendlic and hu lænendlic and hu hreohlic þeos woruld ys.

'now, beloved men, let us remember, as we are asked and taught, how unstable, how transitory, and how tempestuous this world is'

(88) HomU 32 2

leofan men, **utan don**, swa us ðearf is, beon swiðe gemyndige ure agenre þearfe and geþencan gelome, hu læne þis lif is, and hu egeslic se dom is,

'Beloved men, let us be very mindful, as is necessary for us, of our own need and often remember how transitory this life is, and how fearful the judgement is.'

I may add two more examples from Wulfstan. In (90) modal auxiliaries *magan* and *motan* are also found in pairs.[2]

(89) HomU 27 (Nap 30) 14

Ac **utan don**, swa us þearf is, utan god lufian and godes cyrcan weorðian and werian and godes lagum fyligean and ealle ure wisan rædlice fadian.

'But let us do, as is necessary for us, let us love God and worship the church of God, and keep and follow the laws of God and quickly set all our ways in order.'

---

1   These examples of *utan don* may prove the function of anticipatory *don*.

2   See Ogura (2000) for a more detailed explanation.

(90) WHom 3 74

Eala, leofan men, **utan don** swa us þearf is, beorgan us georne wið þæne egesan ⁊ helpan ure sylfra þa hwile þe we magan & motan, þe læs we for-weorðan þonne we læst wenan.

'Lo! Beloved men, let us do as is necessary for us, let us guard ourselves quickly against the terror and help ourselves as long as we are able and allowed to, lest we should pass away when we least expect.'

'*Uton* + infinitive' is not so frequently seen in poetry, but still we have examples.

(91) GenB 839b

      Uton gan on þysne weald innan,
on þisses holtes hleo.

'Let us go into this forest, into the shelter of this wood.'

(92) Sea 117a

Uton we hycgan   hwær \<we\> ham agen,
ond þonne geþencan   hu we þider cumen,

'Let us consider where we should have home, and then think how we should go there'

9.2. Usefulness of the periphrasis

This periphrasis was so limited in time and occurrence that it had a fate to disappear, and 'V^{imp} *we*' outlived it. Meanwhile it took some time for '*let us*' to be spread in place of them. But because of the existence of such a combination *utan don*, we cannot ignore this periphrasis in the early history of the language.

Chapter 10 causative auxiliaries

10.1. Dictionary Data and Additional Data

The two diagrams in Ogura (2002b: 92) may tell the relationship and development of causative, preterite, and inceptive auxiliaries. As causative auxiliaries, *ger* (< ON *gøra*) was used in the North, *make* and *let* in the West, and *did* in the East in the thirteenth century Middle English; *cause* joined in from Old French. Meanwhile *con*, a phonetic variant of *gan*, was used in the North and the West in the same century, while *gan* prevailed in the East and the South. They intermingled in some way but finally developed into periphrastic *did* and inceptive *began* during the Middle English period. Diagrams below are revised from Ogura (2002b: 92).[1]

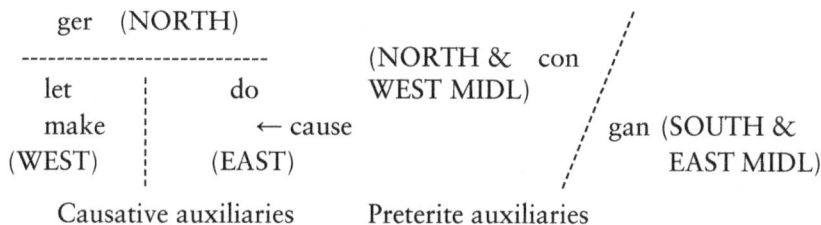

```
     ger   (NORTH)                                      /
   ------------------------      (NORTH &   con        /
     let       ¦      do         WEST MIDL)           /
     make      ¦    ← cause                          /  gan (SOUTH &
    (WEST)     ¦    (EAST)                          /      EAST MIDL)
                                                   /
        Causative auxiliaries    Preterite auxiliaries
```

According to *OED3* **let**, *v.*[1], some earlier examples are quoted in connection with a causative sense of the verb. Under II. Uses requiring a following infinitive (normally without *to*), 12. a. *trans*. Not to prevent; to suffer, permit, allow, three earlier examples can be seen: 971 *Blickl Hom.* 51 *Hwæt dest þu þe gif Drihten .. þe læteþ þone teoþan dæl anne habban*, *a*1100 *Gerefa* in *Anglia* (1886) 9. 260 *Ne læte he næfre his hyrmen hyne ofer wealdan*, and 12. in *Trin.Coll.Hom.* 258 *Let vs, louerd, comen among þin holi kineriche*. Under 13. To cause. Now only in *to let* (**a person**) **know** = to inform (of something), there is an explanatory sentence, which reads "In early use, often with ellipsis of an indefinite personal object, so that the active infinitive has virtually assumed a passive sense; cf. German *lassen*." Earlier examples are: *c*900 tr. Bede *Eccl. Hist.* III. xiv. [xviii.] (Caius) *He sette scole, & on þære he let cnihtas læran*, *a*1123 *Anglo-Saxon Chron.* anno

---

1 A closer investigation on verbs of motion is in Ogura (2002a).

1102 *He let þær toforan castelas gemakian.* Two Middle English examples of '*let* + object + infinitive' are found under II. 14. a.: *c*1386 Chaucer *Man of Law's Tale* 855 *Lat vs stynte of Custance but a throwe, And speke we of the Romayn Emperour* and 1489 (*a*1380) J. Barbour *Bruce* (Adv.) I. 498 *Lat me ta ye state on me And bring yis lans out off thyrllage.* Here I give a few Old English examples of '*lætan* + infinitive', which are quoted in *BT* and *OED3* but following the quotations in *DOE* web corpus.

> (93) Bede 3 (O) 14.208.10
> he sette scole. ⁊ on þære he **let** cnihtas **læran** mid felices fultume þæs bisceopes
> 'he established a school, and in which he let youngmen taught with the help of bishop Felix'

> (94) Num 11.24
> he gegaderode hundseofontig manna of Israhela folce; ða he **let standan** ymbeutan ða eardungstowe
> 'he gathered the seventy men of the Israelites, whom he let stood around the tabernacle'

> (95) ChronC (O'Brien O'Keeffe) 1043.5
> ⁊ raðe þæs se cing **let geridan** ealle þa land þe his modor ahte him to handa
> 'and soon after the king had all the land which his mother owned for his hands conquered'

In Old English only a few examples of '*let us* + infinitive' are attested: e.g. *ÆCHomII, 31–32* 248.228 *Of eorðan we arison. læt us on eorðan gerestan. oð þæt god us eft arære* 'From earth we arose; let us rest in earth, until God raise us again.' In the Bible the subjunctive form seems preferred than the construction with *let* during the medieval period. As seen in *Ps 69* a series of subjunctive forms, which will be replaced by *let* in MnE, appears.

> (96) Ps 69.2–5 [Deus in adiutorrium meum intende. domine ad adiuuandum me festina. Confundantur et reuereantur inimici mei. qui querunt animam meam. Auertantur retrorsum et erubescant qui cogitant mihi mala. Auertantur statim et erubescentes qui dicunt mihi euge euge. Exultent et laetentur qui querunt te domine et dicant semper magnificetur dominus qui diligunt salutare tuum]
> A: god in fultu minne bihald dryhī to gefultumiende me oefesta sien ge-
> scende ⁊ onscunien fiond mine ða ðe soecað sawle mine sien forcerde
> on bec ⁊ scomien ða ðe me yfel sien forcerred sona ⁊ scomiende ða ðe
> cweoðað me weolga weolga gefen ⁊ blissien ða ðe soecað ðæc dryhī ⁊
> cweðen aa sie gemiclad dryhī ða ðe lufiað haelu ðine

D: on fultum minne beheald ⁊ to fylstanne efst ȝescamiȝen ⁊ forwandien
fynd þa ðe secað sawle mine syn acyrred underbeclinȝ ⁊ areodiȝen þa
ðe þencað me yfelu sona ⁊ aryderende þa ðe secȝað eȝlaeȝ upahebben ⁊
blissien þa ðe secað ⁊ cweþen symle sy ȝemiclod þa ðe lufiað hælo þine

I: to minum fultume begem to gefultumianne efest beon gedrefde ⁊ scamian þa þe secaþ mine sawle gecyrran on bæcling ⁊ scamian þa þe willaþ
me yfelu syn afyrsade þærrihte scamiende þa þe secgaþ me eala eala
fægnian ⁊ blissian on þe ealle þa þe sæcaþ þe ⁊ secgan hig symle si
gemærsad drihten þa þe lufiað þinne halwendan

WycEV: God, in to myn helpe tac heed; Lord, to helpen me heeȝe thou. Be
thei confoundid, and shameli drede thei; that sechen my soule. Be thei
turned awei hindward, and waxe thei ashamed; that wiln to mee euelis.
Be thei turned awei anoon and shamende; that seyn to me, Weu! weu!
Ful out ioȝe thei, and glad in thee, alle that sechen thee; and sey thei
euermor; The Lord be magnefied, that loouen thi ȝiuere of helthe.

WycLV: God, biholde thou in to myn heelp; Lord, hast thou to helpe me. Be
thei schent, and aschamed; that seken my lijf. Be thei turned a bak;
and schame thei, that wolen yuels to me. Be thei turned awei anoon,
and schame thei; that seien to me, Wel! wel! Alle men that seken thee,
make fulli ioie, and be glad in thee; and thei that louen thin heelthe,
seie euere, The Lord be magnyfied.

AV: O God, to deliuer mee, make haste to helpe me, O Lord. Let them be
ashamed and confounded that seeke after my soule: let them be turned
backward, and put to confusion, that desire my hurt. Let them be
turned backe for a reward of their shame, that say, Aha, aha. Let all
those that seeke thee, reioyce, and be glad in thee: and let such as loue
thy saluation, say continually, Let God be magnified.

An example of *mak(i)en* as a causative auxiliary in Laȝamon (MS. O). In
OED3 two examles are quoted from the homilies of the transitional period,
one with a bare infinitive and the other with a *to*-infinitive.

(97) Laȝ 9339
C: heo ræsdē to Romleoden: & heo remden to flonne.
O: hii remde to Romlede: and makede heom rugges turne.
'they rushed towards the Romans and they took to flight (and made them
turn their backs)'

(98) LambHom 159.19 (*OED3*)
swa makeð þe halie gast þe .Mon. bi-halden up to houene
'so the Holy Ghost makes the man look up to heaven'

(99) TrinHom 11.23 (*OED3*)
and *þat* is þe deuel. He makeð þe unbilefulle man to leuen swilche wigeles
'and that is the devil; he makes the unbelieving man believe in such divinations'

Causative auxiliaries and *gan/con* periphrases can be found in combination as manuscript variants in *Cursor Mundi*, as in[2]

(100) Cursor 4870
    C: þat al his will **can gar** þe don
    G: þat all his will **can gar** be do
    F: þat alle his wil **con make** be don
    T: And al his wille **con make** be do

(101) Cursor 5323
    C: þe king þan **did** his lettres **writte**
    G: þe king þan **did** his lettris **write**
    F: þe kinge **lete make** his lette*rs* **write**
    T: þe kyng **lete write** lettres ӡare

(102) Cursor 10710
    C: To **do** hir **brek** hir vou, or nai
    G: To **ger** hir **breke** hir vow, or nay
    F: To **make** hir **breke** þat vow or nay
    T: To **make** hir **breke** hir vow or nay

Gart do 'caused someone or something to be done' is also found in *a*1375 *William of Palerne* (Southwest Midland): 3979 *& sche ful godli granted & gart him do fecche* and 5529 *þat gart þis do make* 'who caused this to be done'.

There is another construction peculiar to late Middle English, '*have + don* + infinitive/past participle'. MED **dōn** (v. (1)) 4. (d) gives us examples: (*c*1385) Chaucer CT.Kn. (Manly-Rickert) A. 1913 *An oratorie .. In worship of Dyane .. Hath Theseus doon wroght*, (*a*1393) Gower CA (Frf 3) 4.1836 *He let do yoken gret foxes*, (1465) Paston 4.195 *I have do spoke for yowr worsted*, *a*1475 Siege Troy(1) (Hrl 525) 167/121 *They did do ordeyn for hem-self Good new sheppis*, *a*1500(?*c*1450) Merlin (Cmb Ff.3.11) 57 *The kynge dide do make this dragon*.[3] In Ogura (2003a) I make a report of the combinations *have do make* and *have do and make* in the *Paston Letters*; the latter seems to be preferred in the letters: 199.23 (1467, from Margaret

---

2   Cf. Examples of the manuscript variants of *Cursor Mundi* in Chapter 7.
3   In the preface to the Caxton's translation of *Aneid* (1490) (EETS, e.s. 57 *Caxton Eneydos*) we see the famous story of *egges* and *eyren*, which is quoted by Baugh & Cable (2002:195–6), where we find another example of *did do*: *my lorde abbot of westmynster ded do shewe to me late*.

Paston to John Paston II) *And whan that I haue do and parfourmed that I haue be-gunne I shall purpose me thederward*, 861.15 (1469, from Richard Calle to Margery Paston) *But what, lady, suffer as ye haue do and make you as mery as ye can* (quoted from Ogura (2003a: 9)).

ME *causen* came in rather late. *MED* has the first quotation from Chaucer: (c1385) Chaucer *CT.Kn.* (Manly-Rickert) A.1095 *This prison caused me nat to crye.*

10.2. Usefulness of the periphrasis

This periphrasis is important in combination with the use of preterite auxiliary and the development of periphrastic *do*. The causative verbs we now have are survivors of the syntactic, semantic, and stylistic rivalry in the medieval period.

Chapter 11 modal auxiliaries

11.1. Dictionary Data and Additional Data

Most of the modal auxiliaries which I discuss here in this chapter go back to the Old English preterite-present verbs, i.e. *can, may, must, ought (to), shall*, and an anomalous verb *will*, about the shift of their semantic ranges. Studies I refer to most are Mitchell (*OES*, §§ 990–1024), Mustanoja (1960), and Standop (1957). A very simplified morphological and semantic change of these verbs in historical periods can be illustrated as follows:

OE		ME		MnE
witan/wat 'to know'	→	witen/wot	→	to wiit
cunnan/cuþe 'to know how to'	→	cunnen/coude	→	can/could
magan/meahte/mihte 'to be able to'	→	muwen/mawen/might	→	may/might
motan/moste 'to be allowed to'	→	moten/moste	→	must
sculan/scolde 'to be obliged to'	→	shal/sholde	→	shall/should
agan/ahte 'to have, be obliged to'	→	owen/ouhte	→	owe, own, ought
willan/wolde 'to wish, want to'	→	willen/wolde	→	will/would
durran/dorste 'to dare'	→	durren/dorste	→	dare/dared

Both the similarity and difference of the use of these auxiliaries are attested by the following examples.

(103) GenA 916b
                Nu þu **wast** and **canst,**
lað leodsceaða,   hu þu lifian scealt.
'Now loathsome enemy of men, you know and understand how you shall live.'

(104) Sat 423a
         Nu ic þe halsige,   heofonrices weard,
for þan hirede   þe ðu hider læddest,
engla þreatas,   þæt ic up heonon
mæge and **mote**   mid minre mægðe.
'Now I beseech you, the Guardian of the heavenly kingdom, before the company whom you led here, the hosts of angels, that I might be allowed and permitted to go up from hence with my family.'

(105) El 635
           Is nu worn sceacen,
CC oððe ma   geteled rime.
Ic ne **mæg** areccan,   nu ic þæt rim ne **can.**

'A large amount of time has passed, two hundred (years) or more reckoned in number. I am not able to tell, now that I do not know the number.'

(106) ChristA 246–7

> Us is eallum neod
> þæt we þin medrencynn   motan cunnan,
> ryhtgeryno,   nu we areccan ne mægon
> þæt fædrecynn   fier owihte.

'It is necessary for all of us that we are allowed to know your mother's kindred, the true mistery, now that we are not able to tell (your) father's kin any further.'

(107) Vain 44b

> Nu þu cunnan meaht,
> gif þu þyslicne   þegn gemittest
> wunian in wicum,   wite þe be þissum
> feawum forðspellum   þæt þæt biþ feondes beaarn
> flæsce bifongen,   hafað fræte lif,

'Now you are able to understand, if you find such a thane living in dwellings, beware of yourself by this few intimations, that the son of the enemy will be clad in flesh, have a shameful life,'

(108) Mt 18.24[1] [et cum coepisset rationem ponere oblatus est ei unus qui debebat decem milia talenta]

> Li: ⁊ mið ðy ongann rehtnise setta gebroht wæs him enne seðe **ahte to geldanne** ł tea ðusendo cræftas
> Ru1: ⁊ þa he ingonn gerihtes monige broht wæs him an seþe **scalde** ten þusende
> WSCp: ⁊ þa þe þ gerád sette. him wæs án broht se him **sceolde** tyn þusend punda.
> WycEV: And whanne he began for to putte resoun, oon was offrid to hym, that **owȝte** to hym [LV: **ouȝte**] ten thousand talentis.
> AV: And when hee had begun to reckon, one was brought vnto him which **ought** him ten thousand talents.

---

1 As I explained in Ogura (2007b), it was not 'ought to + infinitive' but 'ought + to-infinitive' that we originally had, and it was not only ought but most preterite-present verbs which ocuured with to as well as without to in early Middle English. It should also be remembered that agan and sculan had been synonymous in the sense 'to owe', and sculan could be used as a full verb: Bod-Hom (Belfour) 34.1–2 Ælc mon eornestlice ah to ȝeldene sum þing, ant hæfð oðerne món þe him sceal sum ðing 'Every man indeed has to pay something, and everyone has another who owes him something.'

(109) GD 1 (C) 4.31.23
7 he þa sona onweg gewat, 7 he na onufan þæt hire gehrinan ne **moste** ne
ne **dorste**
[H: hyre æthrinan ne dorste].
'and he went away, and he in addition to that, was neither allowed nor
dared to touch her'

(110) ÆLS (PrMoses) 64
Se man **mot** hine gebiddan swa swa he **mæg** and **cann**.
forðan þe se ælmihtiga god **cann** ælc gereord tocnawan.
'A man is allowed to pray just as he is able to and knows how to, because
the Almighty God knows how to distinguish every speech.'

(111) ChronE (Irvine) 1137.32
I ne **can** ne I ne **mai** tellen alle þe wunder ne alle þe pines ðat hi diden wrecce
men on þis land;
'I neither know how to nor am able to tell all the horror and all the torments
that they did to the wretched men in this land'

(112) Cursor (C) 27407
Lufand he be nent god and man
Efter þat he **mai** and **can**.

The set of 'Aux + Inf' may fill the half-line and, in most instances, it is
the infinitive that bear alliteration, but in a few examples, like (106), the
auxiliary may alliterate. I investigate these sets and show which has alliteration more often, either the auxiliary (e.g. *Beo* 2083b *gongan wolde*) or
the infinitive (e.g. *PPs* 88.3 2b *wolde gangan*). The result will show that
the more meaningful element, the infinitive, tends to have alliteration.[2] *Met*
and *PPs* maintain their peculiarity.[3]

---

2   Among all poems I here cite those with more examples. Forms investigated
and found examples are: *wile, wille, willað, woldan, wolde, wolden, wold-*
est, woldon, woldun, sceal, sceall, scealt, sceolan, sceoldan, sceolde, sceoldon,
sceoldes, sceoldest, sceolden, mæg, mæge, meahtan, meahte, meahtes, meahton,
mihte, mihten, mihton, moste, mostan, mosten, mostes, moistest, oston, can,
cann, canst, con, const, cunnan, cannaþ, cunne, cunnen, cuðe, cuðon.
3   For the more detailed investigation see Donoghue (1987).

	Inf (allit.) + Aux		Aux (allit.) + Inf	
	a-verse	b-verse	a-verse	b-verse
Beo	10	80		
Gen	10	52		
Met	5	30	1	7
And	2	29		1
Guth	7	27		1
Rid	3	20		1
El	2	20		
Dan	1	20		
Sat	6	18		
PPs	2	18		11
Christ	2	18		
Jul	4	12		1

Auxiliaries, especially *shall* and *will*, were used in the same or similar contexts as manuscript varinats in Laȝamon.

	Calig.	Otho
370	for muchel we wlleð driȝen	for ...... we sollen dreȝen
5770	þe sculleð eow wurðlic he wreken	þat wolleþ ȝou worþlice a-wreke
7358	ȝif þu me wult ilæiuen	Nou þou me miht ilefue
7883	sikerlichen we sculdē uaren	sikerliche mihte ich fare
17404–5	Wel wuste Merlin	Ac wel wiste Merlyn
	hu hit sculde iwurðen.	hou hit wolde iworþe.
21100	and we sculled buȝen	nou we mote wende
21442	nu þu scalt to hælle	ac nou ȝe mote to helle

Sometimes *ich* and *we* or *þu* and *ȝe* could change, and in the next example the giver and the receiver shift in the context.

(113) Laȝ 4707–8
C: bute **he** me **wullen** [wulle?] ȝeuen; þat ich him to-ȝeurne.
'unless he will give me what I ask of him'
O: bute **ich mawe** habbe; þat þe ich ȝeorne.
'unless I may have what I ask you'

'Aux + Inf' often appeared as a variant of a simple verb form, as in[4]

	Calig.	Otho
883-4	ȝif he me ȝefeð gersume	ȝif he vs ȝiue wolle
	gold & seoluer.	gold and garisom.
2423	þe ælc monne abideð	þat ech man mot abide
2691	& ich heo(m) þe wulle nēnen	and ich ȝou telle
5946	þ þe kinges heom speken wið	þat þe kinges wolde speke wi .
13087-8	& aðes ich þe swerie	and ich þe wolle swerie
	þat þis ich wulle uorien.	þat ich þe swike neolle.
14152	ȝif þu þis ȝettest me	ȝef þou þis wolt granti me
14644-5	Þa wes Vortimer	þat hii wolde Vortimer
	cristine kīg þer.	makie cristene king þer.
15683	sæl þe scal iwurðen	leof þou hart me swiþe

'Aux + Inf' and other periphrases can be manuscript variants, as seen in the following examples.

	Calig.	Otho
643	þenne he hit hefde bi-wnnen	wāne he hit mihte awinne
2569	þ he sone dæd wes	þat he solde deȝe
7589	and beo þer wuniende	and þare he wolde abide
11164	þat heo hire scolden ræden	and hii hire gonne reade

The optative use of *may* starts from the sixteenth century, as *OED3* may . 1 12. has it. After the expression in a *that*-clause ([1501]), examples are quoted with VS inversion: 1521 *Petition* in *Hereford Munic. MSS* (transcript) (O.E.D. Archive) I.II.5 *Wherefore it may please you to ennacte* etc.; cf. 1582-3 *Hereford Munic. MSS* (transcript) II.265 *May [it] pleas yo(ur)r worshipes to caule]* and 1570 M. Coulweber in J. W. Burgon *Life & Times Sir T. Gresham* (1839) II.360 *For so much as I was spoyled by the waye in cominge towards England by the Duke of Alva his frebetters, maye it please the Queenes Majestie [etc.].* Under 9.b. In clauses depending on such verbs as *beseech, desire, demand, hope,* and their allied nouns, however, an Old English example which is quite similar to the previous ones: OE Ælfic *Catholic Homilies: 1ˢᵗ Ser.* (Royal) (1997) x.258 *Hwæt wilt ðu þæt ic þe do? He cwæð: drihten þæt ic mæge geseon.* If we accept this as a prototype of an optative use of *may*, we can further say that a gloss might have had

---

4 *Come/come* can be function as auxiliary when used with another verb of motion: 5825 (C) þ we ham cumen liðen; (O) þat we ham wende.

it (**may** *v.* 1, 1.a.): eOE (Mercian) *Vespasian Psalter* (1965) ix.20 [*Exurge domine non praeualeat homo*] *aris dryhten ne meg mon*. Even if this seems far-fetched, a fourteenth century example, under 24. Used (since Middle English with inversion of verb and subject) in exclamatory expressions of wish, can be more appropriate: *c*1325 (?*c*1225) *King Horn* (Harl) (1901) 166 (*MED*) *Crist him myhte blesse*.

Visser (1963–73) has more to say. In his §1680 and in the footnote, which I quote here, he has a quite interesting discussion in relation to the use of subjunctive forms.

> §1680 — Type 'Wo *maye you be* that laughe now!' In this type *may* is used in a pattern which expresses a wish whose realization depends on conditions beyond the power or control of the speaker. The extremely rare occurrence of this usage before the beginning of the sixteenth century[1] is due to the prevalent use in Old English and Middle English of the modally marked form of the verb in this case (e.g. Ælfred, Bede 528, 24, 'ne *forealdige* ðeos hand æfre', *c*1205 Layamon (Brook, Selections) 2591, 'Nu *fulste* us Marie Goddes milde moder'. (See §841, as well as to the use of *mote* + infinitive in Middle English, e.g. *c*1275 Passion Our Lord, in O.E. Misc. 39, 'Iblessed *mote he beo* þe cumeþ on godes nome'; *c*1380 Pearl 397, '*Blysse mote* þe bytyde!' (See §1691)).
>
> [1] As to Old English, the form *mæg* instead of the 'subjunctive' *mæge* clearly shows that the following quotations do not belong here, *pace* Professor Standop (1957 pp. 25–6): Genesis 2661, 'He *abiddan mæg*, gif he ofstum me ærendu wile …'; Christ & Satan (Junius MS., ed. Krapp) 282, 'Forþon *mæg gehycgan*, se ðe hie heorte deah, …'; Ælfred, Boeth. (Sedgefield) 17,14, 'ðu *meaht* ðæs habban ðanc'. Nevertheless Professor R. K. Gordon (Ags. Poetry Selected & Translated, Everym. p. 367) translates Battle of Maldon 314, 'Her lið ure ealdor eal forheawen, god on greote. A *mæg gnornian* se ðe nu fram þis wigplegan wendan þenceð' by '*may he lament* for ever who thinks now to turn from this war-play'.

In fact it is difficult to find the real optative use of OE *mæg* (or *mæge*, if we follow Visser), when the subjunctive form of a verb could be used instead of an auxiliary *magan*. Modern translation can be possible for a subjunctive form of a verb alone, as Clark Hall and Wrenn (1940) do for *Beowulf* 316–318a: *Mæl is me to feran; fæder alwalda mid arstafum eowic gehealde siða gesunde*. '*It is time for me to depart; may the Almighty Father keep you safe in your adventures by His grace.*' It may be also true that such Middle English phrasal expressions as *be as hit may* and *hit may wel be* (e.g. *MED* **mouen** (*v.*(3)) 12.(a), *c*1275 (?*a*1200) Lay. *Brut* (Clg A.9) 32239 *þa ʒet ne* *com þæs ilke dæi; beo heonne uorð alse hit mæi; iwurðe þet iwurðe.*). It should also be remembered that ME *moten* had experienced a fusion with ME *mouen* in the transitional period to produce such constructions as: *c*1275(?*a*1200) Lay. *Brut* (Clg A.9) 4481 *A mote þu wel færen, & Delgan mi dohter* and 22152 *Hal seo þu, Arður .. and þi duȝeðe mid þe – a mote heo wel beo.*[5]

According to *MED*, the 'modal auxiliary + *have* + past participle' construction is attested just before the thirteenth century. Under **haven** (v.) 12c. (c) and (d) there are many: ?*c*1200 *Orm.*(Jun 1) ded.151 *I shall hafenn addledd me þe Laferrd Cristess are, a*1225(?OE) *Lamb.Hom.* (Lamb 487) 11 *Moyses .. feste þes daȝes .. and ec crist hit walde habben idon, a*1250 *Ancr.* (Nero A.14) 47/23 *Muchel hofleas is þet .. vorte sechen .. more lefdischipe þen heo muhte habben iheued [Corp-C: ihaued] .. i ðe worlde, a*1375 *WPal.* (KC 13) 1946 *Amendid in no maner ne miȝt it haue bene.* These examples show no dialectal preference concerning this construction.

11.2. Usefulness of the periphrasis

This is one of the best devices in the history of English to provide writers and readers to convey a subtle shades of meaning in every context it appears. From the very starting point of the written variety, Old English made use of modal auxiliaries as well as subjunctive forms. Since preterite-present verbs could be used as full verbs, *agan* and *sculan* shared the semantic field of possession with *habban*. *Cunnan* might show a semantic overlap with *witan*, but showed more contrast with *magan*. *Motan* developed its way between *sculan* and *magan* in Middle English morphologically and semantically. *Willan* and *wilnian* were synonymous but rarely showed rivalry as auxiliary, while in Middle English texts *willen* and *schulen* developed secular-religeous contrast in their usage. Modal auxilaries have been investigated by a great number of scholars because of their systematic use and semantic shift.

---

5 Matsuse (2015) has a discussion on the development of the *may* optative in full detail. Unfortunately it is in Japanese, and more unfortunately he does not use *OED3* (or was it unavailable when he wrote his first draft?) but only *OED2* throughout, and consequently the numbers of significations differ.

Chapter 12 double modals

12.1. Dictionary Data and Additional Data

In this chapter I mainly discuss double modals. It is true that 'the house is being built' type of construction took a long time to be established, owing to the English feature of a slow development of the combination of the passive + progressive. But this is a general tendency and, when once established, the construction replaced the earlier 'the house is building' in Standard English. The double modal construction, on the other hand, left as a dialectal one in the Southern and Western parts of the U. S. and in the Northern part of England in PDE. One has survived into standard, and the other remained but limited. After I reported this construction in Ogura (1993c), this has become a topic of modern linguists.[1]

As this construction has been widely seen in Germanic languages, it could not have been considered unusual if it had appeared in medieval English. The text which favours this expression is the Wycliffite Bible, but ahead of that, *MED* gives examples from the twelfth century poem *Ormulum*:[2] 3944 *Þatt mannkinn shollde muȝhenn wel Upp cumenn inntill heoffne*, 5286 *& tanne shallt tu muȝhenn sen*, 7301 *Næfr an off hemm Ne shall þær muȝhenn mælenn ȝæn Crist*, and 11445 *He shall muuȝhenn ȝemenn himm*. Then we see examples of *shall (not) mowe*. (I give examples of Old English versions as well, so as to show that this expression was not found in that period.)

> (114) Mk 3.26 [et si satanas consurrexit in semet ipsum dispertitus est et non
>   poterit stare sed finem habet]
>   *Li:*   ꝼ gif l ðeah se wiðerwearda efne arísa on hine sulfne toworpen wæs
>   l bið ꝼ ne mæg gestonde ah ende hæfeð
>   *Ru2:* ꝼ gif æe wiðerworda efne arises in hine solfne to-worpen wæs l bið ꝼ
>   ne mæg gi-stonda ah ende hæfeð
>   *WSCp:* ꝼ gif satanas winð ongen hine sylfne he bið to-dæled ꝼ he standan ne
>   mæg ac hæfð ende
>   *WycEV:* And if Sathanas hath risen aȝeins hym self, he is disparpoilid, and he
>   **shal not mowe stonde,** but hath an ende.

---

1   See also Ogura (1998a).
2   *MED* **mouen** v. (3), 10. (b) and (d).

WycLV: And if Sathanas hath risun aȝens hym silf, he is departid, and he **schal not mowe stonde**, but hath an ende.

AV: And if Satan rise vp against himselfe, and be diuided, hee cannot stand, but hath an end.

(115) Lk 1.20 [Et ecce eris tacens et non poteris loqui usqu*e* in diem quo haec fiant]

Li: ⁊ heono ðu bist suigende ⁊ ne mæge ðu gesprece oðð on doege of ðæm ðas geworðes

Ru2: ⁊ heonu ðu bist swigende ⁊ ne mæge ðu gespreaca oððe on dæge of ðæm ðes worðes

WSCp: And nu þu byst suwiende. ⁊ þu sprecan ne miht. oð þone dæg þe ðas ðing gewurðaþ.

WycEV: And loo! thou shalt be stille, *or doumbe*, and thou **schalt not mowe speke** til in to the day, in which thes thingis schulen be don

WycLV: And lo! thou schalt be doumbe, and thou **schalt not mow speke** til in to the dai, in which these thingis schulen be don

AV: And behold, thou shalt be dumbe, and not able to speake, vntill the day that these things shall bee performed.

It is characteristic of this double modal *shall mowe* to be use mostly in the negative. Many more examples can be found in *Hexateuch* in the Wycliffite.

(116) Ex (Wyc) 33.20
EV: Thou **shalt not mowe** se my face
LV: Thou maist not se my face

(117) Num (Wyc) 31.23
EV: what euer thing fier **shal not mowe** susteyn
LV: what euer thing may not suffer fier

(118) Deut (Wyc) 22.19
EV: he **shal not mowe** leeue hir
LV: he **schal not mowe** forsake hir

It is understandable that, before the borrowing of the word *able* in the middle of the fourteenth century,[3] this construction would be useful. There is an example from Laȝamon's *Brut*.

---

3 The phrase *be able to* is found in Chaucer, as quoted in *MED* **able** (adj.) 1. (b): (c1390) Chaucer *CT. Ph.* (Manly-Rickert) C.134 *Hym thought he was nat able for to speede.*

(119) Laȝ 5744–6

C: Gabius and Ꝑsenna into Lumbardie. / in to þō leode efter monkunne: / þe heom **mihten*** **sculden.** / to helpene heore monne: / aȝen Belinne and Brenne.

O: Gabius and Prosenna. / in to Lombardie hii weren iwend: / after mancunne. / þat mid ȝam solde fihte: / aȝeist Belynes …

[* (Madden's comment) *The second hand has expuncted* mihten, *but perhaps without cause. If any correction is required, we may read* sculen fulsten. Cf. v. 4873.]

Madden's comment suggests that this construction became inappropriate from Modern English viewpoint. We see other combinations in *Cursor Mundi* and the Wycliffite.

(120) Cursor 7701–6

C: And dauid, þat was mild o mode, Again il ai wroght he gode, þat oft-sithes moght he him ha tan And if he **wald him might ha slan**; For fra þe kings aun bedd þus he broght a priue wedd.

G: And dauid þ*a*t was milde of mode, Agaynes euil ay did he gode, þat oft-sith miht him haue tane, And if he **wald miht þai*m*** [*read* him] **haue slane.** For fra þe kinges aun bedd, þus he broght a preue wedd;

F: bot dauid þat was milde of mode agayne þe euel wroȝt þe gode. *and* oft-siþe wiþ mode *and* mayne. *and* he **walde muȝt him haue slaine** for fra þe kinges awen bedde. þus he broȝt a priue wedde.

T: Dauid þ*a*t was milde of mode Dud eu*er* aȝeynes euel þe gode Ofte he **miȝte** saule **haue take** And **slayn** him in his owne sake For fro þe kyngis owne bed þus he brouȝte a p*ri*ue wed.

(121) Jn 15.7 [Si manseritis in me et uerba mea in uobis manserint quod-cumque uolueritis petetis et fiet uobis]

Li: gif gie wunias on mec ⁊ uorda mina in iuih hia gewunias ⁊ suæ huæd gie uælle giuas gie ł biddeð ⁊ bið iuh sald

Ru2: gif ge wunigas in me ⁊ word min in iow ic wunigo swa hwæt ge welle ge giowiga ⁊ bið sald iow

WSCp: Gyf ge wuniað on me ⁊ mine word wuniað on eow. biddað swa hwæt swa ge wyllon ⁊ hyt byð eower

Wyc*EV*: If ȝe schulen dwelle in me, and my wordis schulen dwelle in ȝou, what euere thing ȝe **schulen wilne**, ȝe schulen axe, and it schal be do to ȝou.

Wyc*LV*: If ȝe dwellen in me, and my wordis dwelle in ȝou, what euer thing ȝe wolen, ȝe schulen axe, and it schal be don to ȝou.

AV: If ye abide in me, and my words abide in you, ye shall aske what ye will, and it shall be done vnto you.

Unlike *willan*, *wilnian* had never been used as an auxiliary. The combination *schulen wilne*, therefore, could be simply a confusion of *willan* and *wilnian* (though the confusion is rather rare in Old English). The only example I found and reported in Ogura (1993c) is the construction of this kind, i.e.

(122) GD1 9.61.11

C: Nis hit na þæt Petrus, þæt drihten wolde aht swylces beon ⁊ ne mihte beon, ac he sealed þa bysene mid þy lareowdome his sylfes lare, hwæt his leomu **sceolan wilnian** þæt we wæron, oððe hwæt hi **sceolan nyllan**.

H: Eornostlice drihten nolde na, þæt æni þing swilces gewurde ⁊ hit na beon ne mihte, ac he sealde bysene mid lareowdome his sylfes lare, hwæt his limu **scylon gewilnian**, oððe hwæt eac be him **nellendum gewurðan sceoldon**.

Nyllan is a shortened form of *ne willan*, not *ne wilnian*, but it is quite likely that the two verbs were in confusion and produced a nearly double modal situation. From these examples, it can be true that some texts under northern influences showed these combinations of modals and the remnants can be seen dialectally in PDE.

12.2. Usefulness of the periphrasis

Grammatically this periphrasis is not at all useful in the present-day Standard English, but historically it was, and dialectally it has been useful in expression a subtle shades of meaning by the combination of the two modal auxiliaries.

Chapter 13 'impersonals' and 'reflexives'

13.1. Dictionary Data and Additional Data

In terminology I have always been mindful of differentiating 'impersonal'[1] and impersonal (without single quotes); the latter is mostly of natural phenomena, like *it rains* or *it thunders*, which never occurs with the dative of person, while the former almost always takes the dative of person, like *it pleases me* or *it seems better for him*, and possesses the chance of shifting into a personal construction. We may simply choose a personal construction, therefore, and say *he thinks* and do not need to say *it seems to him*, but there must be some nuance when we use two kinds of expressions. In the same way, 'reflexive' should be differentiated from reflexive (without single quotes); the latter means a real reflexive, like *behave yourself*, but the former is a typically medieval one, in which the coreferential pronoun appears in all four cases, either with or without *self* inflecting in the same case, like *he him gewat* or *ich ondræd me*, and *he cwæð to him selfum*

---

1 The use of single quotes on 'impersonal' as a term is my devise. As seen in Gaaf (1904), constructions with the dative of person have a possibility either to shift into personal constructions or to remain 'impersonal' after being marked by the preposition *to* or *for*. Once the dative of person is represented by *to* and branded as ex-dative, the construction itself cannot become personal. For instance, *me þyncð* cannot be shifted to *I think* straightway, once *me* is identified as the dative by *to*; *it seems to me* cannot be shifted to *I think* or *I seem* straightway (I am now explaining the process skipping the morphological fusón between *þyncan/ þuht(e)* and *þencan/þoht(e)* and the borrowing of *seem* from Old Norse). When I was in Oxford and studied under the direction of Bruce Mitchell back in 1983, he asked me why I used the inverted commas to the term impersonal. I explained him this historical process in detail and he seemed to understand me. After the publication of *OES*, I found the note in his General Index (1985: 817): "*Note: I regret that I have not consistently observed the strict definition of 'impersonal' proposed in §1025; see, for example, §§ 1251 and 1349. In these and similar contexts, the word should be in inverted commas.*" Though my name is not mentioned, the use of inverted commas to 'impersonal' is my original idea. As for 'reflexive', it is also my device. See also an old but important book by Wahlén (1925).

cannot be morphologically defined as reflexive or not without considering the context. The first example of 'he said to himself' is found in Laȝamon.[2]

(123) Laȝ 1537

    C: Corineus com quecchen: & **to him seolfe queð**.
    A-wæi Corineus: nere þu icoren kempa.
    O: Corineus com scecky: and **seide to him seolue**.
    Awac Corineus: nere þou icore kempe.

The earliest example of both 'impersonal' and reflexive is found in *CP(H)*, one an 'impersonal' and reflexive use of OE *ðyncan* with a *þæt*-clause and the other a personal and reflexive use of OE *ðyncan* (or a fusion with *ðencan*) with adjectives.

(124) CP(H) 17.112.10–12

    Ærest **him ðuhte selfum** ðæt ðæt he were swiðe unmedeme, ac siððan he understungen ⁊ awreðed wæs mid ðys hwilendlecan onwalde, he **ðuhte him selfum** swiðe unlytel ⁊ swiðe medeme.
    'As first he himself thought that he was incompetent, but when he was supported by transitory authority, he considered himself far from despicable and quite competent.'
    (tr. by Sweet)

Examples in late OE Ælfric are (125) 'impersonal' where him is reinforced by sylfum, and (126) and (127) with and without *sylf-*. In ME *Cursor Mundi* we find 'impersonal' and reflexive.

(125) ÆCHom II, 19 174.23

    ac **him sylfum getimode** swa swa he ðam oðrum gemynte
    'but it happened to him as he intended for the other'

(126) ÆCHom II, 28 226.170

    Ofer **me sylfne** ic getimbrige mine cyrcan. ofer **me** ic getimbrige ðe. na me ofer ðe.
    'Over myself I will build my church; over me I will build thee, not me over thee.'

---

2   *MED* has an example of 'say to thyself': c1175(?OE) *Bod.Hom.* (Bod 343) 124/6 *Ac loca þenne on þa buriȝnes ⁊ sæȝ to þe sylfum, 'Hwæt! þæs món iu on þissre worlde wunsumlice lyfede þe ic ær cuðe.'* 'But look then on the grave and say to thyself, 'Lo, this man whom I used to know, of old lived happily in this world' (trans. by Belfour).

(127) ÆCHom II, 33 250.25
Ælc man ðe hine godne talað and oðre forsihð. bið fram gode forsewen.
swa swa se sunderhalga wæs. þe hine sylfne ðurh agenum geearnungum
godne tealde. and ðone oðerne hyrwde;
'Everyone, who accounts himself good and neglects others, will be neglected
from God, as the Pharisee was, who through his own merits accounted
himself good and neglected others.'

(128) Cursor 27339
C: Be-hald noght in þe ei þat hir thinc scam hir-self to wrei;
F: be-halde þe womman noʒt in þe eye. þat hir þink shame hir-seluin wrey.
'Do not behold the woman in the eye, in that it would seem to her a
shame to accuse herself.'

Both constructions shifted syntactically as well as morphologically and lexi-
cally to survive the history of the language. The process can be exemplified
in the following diagram.

he gewat him   →   he went
he gecyrde him   →   he turned himself / he turned around
he ondræd him   →   he feared / he was afraid
he sægde him   →   he said to him   ↔   he said to himself
he eaðmedde him   →   he humbled /prostrated himself
him gelamp   →   it happened to him
me þuhte   →   me thought   →   methought
                  it seemed to me ↔ I thought
him licode   →   it pleased him   ↔   he liked
him hyngreþ / him is hungrig   →   he is hungry
him nedeþ   →   it needs him   →   it is nessesary for him

Because of the fact that, especially in Old English poetry, the thing or event,
rather than the person, was stylistically selected as the subject, like *Beo* 447b
gif mec deað nimeð or 473a *Sorh is me to secganne*, the 'impersonal' construction survived into late medieval period or beyond. The 'reflexive' construction survived as well, partly reinforced by the Old French use of personal
pronoun alone as the reflexive pronoun, until in the late fifteenth century the
element *self* became firmly combined with the personal pronoun.

13.2. Usefulness of these periphrases

In Modern English the 'impersonal' construction remains as a variant of the
personal construction or as an idiomatic expression like *as you like/please*.
The 'reflexive' construction, especially without *self*, is ousted by the real

reflexive. Since 'impersonals' and 'reflexives' were typical in Old English syntax and continued to be used in Middle English, they must be indispensable in early English. 'Impersonal', 'personal' (i.e. with nominative of thing or event) and personal were alternatives, even though sometimes not all three of them could be seen in extant texts, and after syntactic, semantic and stylistic conflict the personal construction has become predominant. 'Reflexive' constructions, i.e. with coreferential pronouns, had a chance to occur with any verb, but again there had been some traits to take either with or without *self*. As an indefinite pronoun that functioned adjectivally and agreed with the co-occurring personal pronoun, *self* demanded, though not always, an alliterating position in Old English poems, appeared in prepositional phrases in the Middle English alliterative long lines, but it was Chaucer's time when *self* was finally secured its combination with the personal pronoun. Both constructions with or without *self* were used in environmental distribution in medieval texts.

Chapter 14 'preposition + noun' and verb-adverb combinations

14.1. Dictionary Data and Additional Data

The use of preposions has been considered as the sign of the shift from synthetic early English to analytic Modern English. It is a well-known fact that a preposition originally governed the case or cases of a noun, not being combined with a verb. Owing to the morphological ambiguity prepositions became more and more useful, but from the very beginning of the English language the choice between a simple noun and 'preposition + noun' was optional to some extent; moreover, the choice of prepositions also varies. Thus we find such examples as

(129) Ps 6.7 [lacrimis stratum meum rigabo]
   A: mid tearum strene mine ic wetu
   D: of tearum stræle mine ic lecce ł wæte
   G: tearum miñ [meis] strewene miñ ic lǽcce
 AV: I water my couch with my tears.

(130) Ps 29.11 [Conuertisti planctum meum in gaudium mihi conscidisti saccum meum et praecinxisti me letitia]
   A: Ðu gecerdes wop minne in gefean me ðu toslite sec minne ⁊ bigyrdes me mid blisse
   D: Ðu gecyrdest heof minne on gefean ðu slite heran mine ⁊ ðu begyrdest of blisse
   E: Ðu gecirdest minne heof on gefeæn me þu tostlite ł curfe mine sęc ł hæran ⁊ me begierdest me on blisse
   F: Þu gecyrdest heof minne on gefean me þu slite hæran mine ⁊ þu ymbsealdest [circumdedisti] me blisse
   I: Þu gecerdest ł þu ahwyrfdest ł þu awendest wop minne ł mine heofunge to blisse ł on gefean me þu toslite sæc minne ⁊ þu ymbsealdest ł ymbsettest [circumdedisti] me mid blisse
 AV: Thou hast turned for mee my mourning into dauncing: thou hast put off my sackecloth, and girded mee with gladnesse

It is interesting to see that in (130) *in gaudium* is rendered with a preposition, though it can be *in* or *on* or *to*, and *letitia* can be either preposed by *mid* or *of* or *on* or by none. When the Latin original has a preposition, glossators may feel rather obliged. When there is no preposition in the original, however, they can feel free to use a preposition that governs the case of the noun, or use just a noun with the case ending.

Preposition *to* is used with the indirect object in PDE, but the use was optional during the medieval period. In the Earlier Version of the Wycliffite Bible, we find a too cautious use of *to*, which shows the attitude of identifying ex-datives.[1]

(131) Mt 25.42 [esurivi enim et non dedistis mihi manducare sitivi enim et non dedistis mihi potum]

EV: Sothely I hungeryde, and ȝe ȝauen nat **to** me for to ete; I thristide, and ȝee ȝauen nat **to** me for to drynke;

LV: For Y hungride, and ȝe ȝauen not me to ete; Y thristide, and ȝe ȝauen not me to drynke;

(132) Gen 12.3 [benedicam benedicentibus tibi et maledicam maledicentibus tibi]

EV: and I shal blis **to** thoo that blissen thee, and I shal curse **to** thoo that cursen thee;

LV: Y schal blesse hem that blessen thee, and Y schal curse hem that cursen thee.

(133) Jn 12.44 [qui credit I me non credit in me sed in eum qui misit me]

EV: He that bileueth in **to** me, bileueth not in **to** me, but in **to** him that sente me.

LV: He that bileueth in me, bileueth not in me, but in hym that sente me.

---

1 See Ogura (2018) in detail. I may call a 'prepositon' in early English an 'ex-case indicator'. Here I give a table which shows the cases governed by Old English prepositions, consulting Mitchell (1985; *OES* §1175).

genitive	andlanges, utan
dative	beæftan, begeondan, beneoþan, endlange, foran, fram, of, oninnan, onmiddan, onuppan, samod, toeacan, toefnes/toemnes, togean(es), wiþinnan
accusative	onforan, ufan, ufenan, wiþer
gen. & acc.	andlang
gen. & dat	toforan, toweard(es)
dat. & acc.	abutan, æfter, ær, æt, be, beforan, behindan, betweoh/betweonum/betweox, binnan, bufan, butan, for(e), gemang, geond, in, innan, into, mid, ofer, on, onbutan, ongean, ongemang, onufan, oþ, þurh, þurhut, under, uppan, wiþutan, ymb, ymbutan
gen. & dat. & acc.	to, wiþ

These examples may give modern readers an impression of the ungrammatical use of *to* in *EV*. It is true that in most instances *LV* looks modern. In the following example, however, we see that *EV* has a modern syntax.

(134) Mk 11.26 [quod si vos non dimiseritis nec Pater vester qui in caelis est dimittet vobis peccata vestra]

EV: That if ȝe schulen not forȝyue, neither ȝoure fadir that is in heuenes, schal forȝyue ȝou ȝoure synnes.

LV: And if ȝe forȝyuen not, nether ȝoure fadir that is in heuenes, schal forȝyue to ȝou ȝoure synnes.

We can say nothing sure of the word order as long as we use biblical texts based on the translation of Latin, but we can see how Wyclif used the preposition *to* in his work in explaning *Paternoster* by each passage in the following quotation (the boldface here in this quotation is from the EETS edition).

(135) The English Works of Wyclif (EETS, o.s. 74) p. 198, line 4 to p. 200, line 10
Ȝeue to vs to-day oure eche dayes bred. & forȝeue to vs oure dettis, þat is oure synnys, as we forȝeuen to oure detouris, þat is to men þat han synned *in* vs. ...... Whanne we seyn, & **for-ȝeue vs oure dettis**, þat is oure synnes, **as we forȝeuen to houre dettouris**, þat is to men þat han trespassed aȝenst vs, we [MS. he] preien þat god haue mercy on vs as we han mercy on hem þat han wraþþid vs.

In explaining the preceding passage from *Paternoster*, he uses 'give to us' and 'forgive to us our debts', but in the later explanation he uses 'forgive us our debts' and 'forgive to our debtors'. Both the use of '*to* + indirect object' and the order between the direct object and the indirect object could not, or should not, be judged from the viewpoint of PDE.

Prefixes either put an additional sense to a verb or could be interchangeable. When two prefixes were found, they should be analysed as a combination of a free morpheme (adverb) and a bound morpheme (prefix). As I proposed five stages of the development of the particle-prefix-verb combination to the verb-adverb combination in Ogura (1998b and again in 2002b), this process can be regarded as the development of another periphrastic construction.

Stage 1	(Pa) — P — V	(up)ahebban	(ofer)becuman
		uphebban	ofercuman
Stage 2	P — V — (Pa)	ahebban (up)	becuman (ofer)
		uphebban	ofercuman
Stage 3	(P) — V — (Pa)	(a)hebban (up)	(be)cman (ofer)
		(up)hebban	(ofer)cuman

| Stage 4 | V — (Pa) | hebban (up) | cuman (ofer) |
| Stage 5 | V — Pa | hebban up | cuman ofer |

N. B. V = verb (stem), P = prefix, (P) = an optional prefix, Pa = particle (which may function as a prefix when preposed to V), (Pa) = an optional particle.

It is not obligatory for each verb to start from Stage 1 and end at Stage 5. In extant texts we find fragmental evidence of these stages. If a verb is lucky enough to have diachronic examples of each stage, then we call the phenomenon the development from a prefixed verb to a verb-adverb combination. But it is also true that more than one stage can be seen as manuscript variants, sometimes disregarding chronological development.

(136) Ps 93.2 [Exaltare qui iudicas terram redde retributionem superbit]
  A: **hefe up** ðu doemes eordan ageld edlean oferhygdgum
  D: **ahefe** ðe þu ðe demst eorðan ȝyld edlean ofermodum
  G: **upahefe** þu þe demst eorðan agyld eadlean ofermodum
  AV: Lift vp thy selfe, thou iudge of the earth: render a reward to the proud.

(137) GD2(C) 94.12
  Her **yrneð up** [H: **uppyrneð**] se æftra stream þære ȝodcundan spræce,
  'Here runs up the second stream of the sacred speech'

The gloss to the *Vespasian Psalter* (A) must go back to the middle of the ninth century and that to the *Vitellius Psalter* (G), a D-type psalter, was written in the moiddle of the eleventh century. Both manuscripts of the Gregory's *Dialogues* date sometime in the eleventh century. The chronological order, therefore, does not always match with the supposed development. This means that the prefix-verb and the verb-particle could be stylistic variants in Old English.

14.2. Usefulness of these periphrases

Prepositions were optional in Old English contexts, as long as inflectional endings were unambiguous. Since most prepositions had an adverbial function, it was probable for them to be postposed. When there was a sequence of 'Part + Prefix + V', Part could be postposed and Prefix could be reduced or disappeared, and then 'V + Part' could come out. The first monograph I came up with concerning prefixes to verb-adverb combinations not being based on a specific linguistic theory was Hiltunen (1983). Even though the data was limited, his way of investigation stimulated both philological and linguistic studies on this matter in the following decades.

Chapter 15 periphrases died out in the medieval period

While translating Latin, the Anglo-Saxons invented some calques using their ordinary verbs in a foreign syntax. There were three major expressions: *nelle þu / nællaþ ge* for *noli / nolite, cwyst þu / sægst þu / wenst þu* for *num(quid)*, and *is gecweden* for *dictum est* and *is gelefed* for *licet*. The first type was used as an alternative construction to a negative imperative, the second one for a rhetorical question which presupposes a negative answer, and the third for renderings of perfective, deponent, and 'imperonal' constructions of Latin. These periphrases had gone away from the main road of the linguistic history, because they were calques.

Nole (= *ne + volle*) 'to be unwilling' is used in the second person singular and plural, *noli* and *nolite*, which are literaly translated to *nelle* and *nællaþ* of *nellan* (= *ne + willan*).

When the versions of the Gospels are compared, we find that '*nelle/ nællaþ* + (subject ronoun) + infinitive' was used until Wycliffite, but even in Old English versions the alternative imperative costructions were chosen, and moreover, modal auxiliaries like *sculan* and *þurfan* took place in this construction.[1]

(138) Mt 1.20 [noli timere accipere mariam coniugem tuam]
   Li: nelle ðu ðe ondrede ł forth bian to onfoanne maria gebede ł geoc ðin
   Ru1: ne ondréd þu þe onfoh ł onfoiæ maria wife þinum
   WSCp: nelle þu ondrædan marian þine gemæccean to onfonne
   WycEV: nyl thou drede to take Marie, thi wyf
   Tyn: feare not to take vnto the Mary, thy wife
   AV: feare not to take vnto thee Mary thy wife

(139) Mt 10.9 [nolite possidere aurum neque argentum neque pecuniam in zonis uestris]
   Li: nallas ge agnege gold ne sulfer ne feh on gyrdilsum iurum
   Ru1: ne sculon ge agan góld ne sylfur ne feoh in gyrdels eowrum
   WSCp: næbbe ge gold ne seolfer ne feoh on eowrum bigyrdlum
   WycEV: Nyl ʒe welden gold, nether syluer, ne money in ʒoure girdlis

---

1 For detailed investigation of this construction see Ogura (1988a).

Tyn: **Posses nott** golde, nor silver, nor brasse yn youre gerdels
AV: **Prouide neither** gold, nor siluer, nor brasse in your purses

(140) Mk 6.50 [confidite ego sum **nolite timere**]
    Li: gelefes ic am **nallað ge** ondrede
    Ru2: ic hitt am **nallon ge** ondreda
    WSCp: Gelyfaþ ic hit eom. **ne þurfon ge eow** ondrædan
    WycEV: Triste ʒe, I am; **nyle ʒe drede**
    Tyn: Be of good chere, it is I; **be not afrayed**
    AV: Be of good cheere, It is I, **be not afraid.**

Num(quid), in contrast with *nonne* which in most instances is translated by a combination *hu ne*, *hu nu*, *ah ne*, etc., is rendered into *cwyst þu*, *segst þu*, *wenst þu* (or wenstu), or *is þes wen*, which may mean 'do you say', 'do you think' or 'probably'. This is because OE *cweðan*, *secgan* and *wenan* were ordinary verbs of saying and thinking, and the VS cluster with these verb forms might be useful as an interrogative adverb.[2]

(141) Jn(WSCp) 18.17 [**numquid** et tu ex discipulis es hominus istius]
    cwyst ðu, eart ðu of ðyses learningcnihtum;

(142) Lk(WSCp) 6.39 [**num-quid** potest caecum caecum ducere **nonne** ambo in foueam cadent]
    Segst þu, mæg se blinda þæne blindan lædan; **Hu ne** feallaþ hig begen on þære pytt?

(143) Bo 5.12.31 ["**Num** me," inquit, "fefellit abesse aliquid, per quod, velut hiante valli robore, in animum tuum perturbationum morbus inrepserit?]
    Wenstu þæt ic hyte <þone> dem þinre gedræfednesse þe þu <mid> ymb-fangen eart?

(144) PsGlE 77.19 [**nunquid** poterit deus parare mensam in deserto]
    is þies wen miege god geærwigæn misæn on westnesse

Latin *dictum est*, *uide(a)tur* or *uisum est*, *beneplacitum est*, *decet*, and *licet* were rendered into '*is/wæs* + past participle of an 'impersonal' verb', which had a misnomer of 'impersonal passive'. This was a device for translating Latin deponent verbs or the perfect passive indicative of verbs used imper-sonally. In Old English, because of this device, synonymous verbs with the same syntactic environment were used in glosses and ordinary prose, and further in some poems.[3] Here are some examples.

---

2 For detailed investigation of this construction see Ogura (1984).
3 For detailed investigation of this construction see Ogura (1986b).

(145) Mt 5.31 [Dictum est autem quicumque dimiserit uxorem suam det illi libellum repudii]

    Li: acueden is uutedlice sua hua forletas wif his selle hir boc freodomes

    Ru1: gecwæden wæs þonne swa hwa swa forletae his wif selle him boec þare áweorpnisse

    WSCp: Soðlice hit ys gecweden swa hwylc swa his wif forlæt. he sylle hyre. hyra híwgedales bóc

    WycEV: Forsothe it is said [LV: And it hath be seyd], Who euere shal leeue his wyf, ʒeue he to hir a libel, *that is, a litil boke of forsakyng.*

    AV: It hath beene said, Whosoeuer shall put away his wife, let him giue her a writing of diuorcement.

(146) Mt 18.12 [Quid uobis uidetur si fuerint alicui centum oues et errauerit una ex eis]

    Li: huæt iuh is gesene ┼ g[e]ðence gif he biðon ┼ weron ængum hundrað scipa ⁊ geduologia án of ðæm

    Ru1: hwæt ðincaþ eow gif hæbbe hwa hundteontig scípa ⁊ gedwalige an of ðara

    WSCp: Hwæt ys eow geþuht gyf hwylc mann hæfð hund sceapa. ⁊ him losað án of þam.

    WycEV: What semeth to ʒou? Ʒif ther weren to summan an hundred sheep, and oon of hem shall erre [LV: hath errid],

    AV: How thinke yee? if a man haue an hundred sheepe, and one of them be gone astray,

(147) Ps 146.11 [Beneplacitum est domino super timentis eum]

    A: wel gelicad is driht̄ ofer ondredende hine

    C: welʒelicod ys drihtne ofyr ondrædynde hine

    E: Wellicunga is dryhtene ofer ondriedende hine

    I: gecwemedlic is drihtne ofer þa ondrædendan hine

    J: gecweme is drihtne ofer drædendum hine

WycEV:Wel plesid thing is to the Lord vpon men dredende hym

    AV: The Lord taketh pleasure in them that feare him.

(148) Mt 3.15 [sine modo sic enim decet nos implere omnem iustitiam]

    Li: buta tua suæ forðon gedæfnad is us þ̄ we gefylle alle soðfæs[t]nisse

    Ru1: lét þus nu forðon ðe þus we sculon gefyllan æghwilce soþfæstnisse

    WSCp: Læt nu. þus unc gedafnað ealle rihtwisnesse gefyllan.

    WycEV: Suffre now, for so it becummeth vs [LV: it fallith to vs] for to fulfille all riʒtwisnesse.

    AV: Suffer it to be so now: for thus it becommeth vs to fulfill all righteousnesse.

(149) Mt 19.3 [si licet homini dimittere uxorem suam quacumque ex causa]

    Li: gif is rehtlih ðæm menn forleta wif his ⁊ sua huele ┼ buta eghuelc inðing

87

Ru1:	**mót mon for-letan** wif his for ænegum intinge
WSCp:	**is alyfed** ænegum menn hys wif to forlætenne for ǽnegum þinge
WycEV:	**Wher it be leeful for a man** for to leeue, *or forsake*, his wijf, of what euer cause?
WycLV:	**Whether it be leueful to a man** to leeue his wijf, for ony cause?
AV:	**Is it lawfull for a man** to put away his wife for euery cause?

In these renderings we find such modal auxiliaries as *sculan* and *motan* in addition to the contrasting use of '*is/wæs* + past participle' and the simple form of verbs. It is also noticeable to find an adjectival form, which stem goes back to a personal verb like *gecweman*. These constructions seemed acceptable, when similar constructions were found in poems, as in

(150) And 549a

Huru **is gesyne,** sawla nergend,
þæt ðu þissum hysse hold gewurde
ond hine geongne geofum wyrðodest,
wis on gewitte ond wordcwidum.

'Indeed it is clear, the Saviour of souls, that you have been gracious to this young man, wise in understanding, and honoured him with gifts and speech.'

(151) GuthB 1016b

Is me on wene **geþuht,**
þæt þe untrymnes adle gongum
on þisse nyhtstan niht bysgade,
sarbennum gesoht.

'It seems to me, in my opinion, that the weakness by the attacks of disease in the last night afflicted you, visited you with painful wounds.'

(152) GuthA 612

Þæt **eow** æfre ne **bið** ufan **alyfed**
leohtes lissum, þæt ge lof moten
dryhtne secgan, ac ge deaðe sceolon
weallendne wean wope besingan,
heaf in helle, nales herenisse
halge habban heofoncyninges.

'It shall never be granted to you from above in joys of heaven, that you were able to speak praise to the Lord, but you must sing surging misery in death and in lamentation, wailing in hell, must not have holy praise of the King of heaven at all.'

Chapter 16 Conclusion

The tendency of using periphrastic expressions in order to avoid morphological ambiguity must have started before Old English appeared in extant written documents. The Anglo-Saxons needed to express precisely what they wanted to say, interpret, and record.

Periphrastic expressions in the medieval period made early English enriched in syntactic and stylistic varieties so as to record their own literature as well as to translate religious texts and represent the original meaning. It is also noticeable that medieval scribes know both how to be explanatory in using the periphrastic constructions and how to cut things shorter and clearer. In Gregory's *Dialogues* we often compare MSS CCCC 322 and Hatton 76 (as MS Cotton Otho C.i. vol. 2 is too short for comparison) and find the latter, the revised version, make the context shorter and more concise in some way, even though they were both written in the eleventh century. The revised version sometimes uses infinitives instead of (*that-*) clauses, omits 'impersonal' set-phrase (like *hit gelamp* and *me þincþ*) or 'reflexive' *self* (like *selfum* in *me selfum þynceþ*), which is not so significant in contexts, e.g.

(153) GDPref 1 (C) 6.34
Ac nu þa þe ic ymb sprece, ic gecyðe bet, **me þinceð**, gif ic asceade mid mearcunge þara namena,
GDPref 1 (H) 6.33
Ac þa þing, þe ic ymbe sprece, ic eallunga bet gecyðe, gyf ic mid mearcunge tosceade þara naman,

(154) GD 1 (C) 9.63.4
On þære wisan, Petrus, **us is to gehycganne**, hu mycelne ege **we sceolon witan** to ðam halgum werum, þa syndon Godes templu.
GD 1 (H) 9.63.4
On þam þinge, Petrus, is to geþenceanne, hu micel ege si to hæbbenne to þam halgum werum.

(155) GD 1 (C) 9.66.4
Eac **hit gelamp** on sum tid, þæt him common twegen men to of Gotena þeode, þa sædon, þæt hi to Rauennan faran woldon.

GD 1 (H) 9.66.4

Soðlice on oðrum timan him comon to twegen men of Gotena þeode, þa
sædon, þæt hi to Rauennam faran woldon.

(156) GD 2 (C) 10.123.17

Ða gelamp hit, þæt in gesyhþe godcundan weres gelicode, þæt he het adle-
fan in þære ylcan stowe eorðan for sumre neodþearfe, ˥ þa <hie> þa eorðan
delfende deoppor ofdune becomon, þa gebroðru fundon þær sum æren
feondgyld, ˥ þa awurpon hie þæt to sumre hwile in þa cycenan.

GD 2 (H) 10.123.17

Ða gelicode þam Godes were, þæt hi on þære ylcan stowe dulfon þa eorðan.
˥ þa þa hi deoppor delfende neoðor becomon, þa fundon þa broðru þær
sum æren deofolgyld. þa to sumre hwile awurpon hi hit in to hyra kicenan.

(157) GD 2 (C) 35.174.18

me sylfum þynceð, þæt ic na ne ongyte fornytlice ˥ nydþearflice þa word,
þe þu sædest,

GD 2 (H) 35.174.16

me þinceð, þæt ic full nyttlice ne undergite na þa þing, þe þu sædest,

It can be roughly said that a morphological change started in the final con-
tinuation of the *Peterborough Chronicle*, a lexical change in *Ancrene Riwle*,
a stylistic change in Laȝamon's *Brut*, a syntactic change in *Cursor Mundi*. A
written style was influenced by Anglo-French and Old French, while spoken
variety accepted Old Norse influence. The "Old Englishness" cannot be
defined clearly unless we find the whole remaining texts, but it took more
or less six centuries for the English language to take in some periphrastic
expressions of the predecessors' device, and cast off and replace the other.

From the late twentieth century, studies of Old and Middle English have
made a great progress. In addition, computer corpora have become a quick
and useful tool to find examples in enormous data, even though limited in
comparison with PDE. Using these corpora with syntactic tags, however,
might lead to a danger of grabbing treasures in virtual reality. Even *OED2*,
OED3, *DOE* and *MED* are not so mutually informative, we are living in
the process of compiling data of the medieval English, and there is enough
room for different interpretations of a specific example.

Select Bibliography [with abbreviated titles]

Dictionaries

An Anglo-Saxon Dictionary, eds. Joseph Bosworth and T. N. Toller. 1898; rpt. London: Oxford University Press, 1972. [*BT*]

A Concise Anglo-Saxon Dictionary, ed. J. R. Clark Hall with a Supplement by Herbert D. Meritt. 1894, 4th ed. 1960; rpt. Toronto: University of Toronto Press, 1996. [*CHM*]

Dictionary of Old English, comp. Ashley C. Amos, Antonette diPaolo Healey, *et al.* Toronto: Pontifical Institute of Medieval Studies, University of Toronto, 1988–. *DOE Web Corpus* http://tapor.library.utoronto.ca/ [*DOE*]

Historical Thesaurus of Oxford English Dictionary, with Additional Material from 'A Thesaurus of Old English', eds. Christian Kay, Jane Roberts, Michael Samuels, Irené Wotherspoon. Oxford: Oxford University Press, 2009. [*HTOED*]

The Kenkyusha Dictionary of English Etymology, eds. Yoshio Terasawa, *et al.* Tokyo: Kenkyusha, 1997.

A Middle English Dictionary, eds. Hans Kurath, Sherman Kuhn, *et al.* Ann Arbor: University of Michigan Press, 1956–2000. http://quod.lib.umich.edu/m/med/ [*MED*]

The Oxford English Dictionary, 2nd edition, eds. John A. Simpson and Edmund S. C. Weiner. Oxford: Clarendon Press, 1989. *OED 3rd edition* www.oed.com [*OED3*]

A Thesaurus of Old English, comp. Jane Roberts and Christian Kay with Lynne Grundy, 2 vols. King's College London Medieval Studies XI, 1995.

Toller, T. N. (ed.) 1921. *An Anglo-Saxon Dictionary. Supplement* with *Revised and Enlarged Addenda* by Alistair Campbell. London: Oxford University Press, 1973. [*BTS*]

Concordance

A Concordance to Anglo-Saxon Poetic Records, eds. J. B. Bessinger, Jr. and Philip H. Smith, Jr. Ithaca and London: Cornell University Press.

Translations

Bradley, S. A. J. (tr. & ed.) 1982. *Anglo-Saxon Poetry*. The Everyman Library. London: Dent.

Clark Hall, John R. (tr. & ed.) 1911. *Beowulf and the Finnesburg Fragment*. Completely revised by C. L. Wrenn with prefatory remarks by J. R. R. Tolkien. Northampton: George Allen & Unwin, 1940, 1950.

Garmonsway, G. N. (tr. & ed.) 1953. *The Anglo-Saxon Chronicle*. rpt. London: Dent & Sons, 1972.

Editions

Bately, Janet. (ed.) 1980. *The Old English Orosius*. EETS, s.s. 6. London: Oxford University Press. [*Or*]

–. 1986. *The Anglo-Saxon Chronicle. A Collaborative Edition*. Vol. 3, MS. A. Cambridge: D. S. Brewer. [*ChronA*]

Behaghel, Otto. (ed.) 1882. *Heliand und Genesis*. 10th Aufl. von Burkhaut Taeger. Tübingen: Max Niemeyer, 1996.

Belfour, A. O. (ed.) 1909. *Twelfth-Century Homilies in MS. Bodley 343*. EETS, o.s. 137. rpt. London: Oxford University Press, 1962. [*BodHom*]

Bethurum, Dorothy. (ed.) 1957. *The Homilies of Wulfstan*. Oxford: Clarendon Press. [*WHom*]

Bosworth, Joseph, and G. Waring. (eds.) 1888. *The Gothic and Anglo-Saxon Gospels in Parallel Columns with the Versions of Wycliff and Tyndale*. London: Reeves & Turner. [*Tyn*]

Brooks, Kenneth R. (ed.) 1961. *Andreas and the Fates of the Apostles*. London: Oxford University Press.

Clemoes, Peter. (ed.) 1997. *Ælfric's Catholic Homilies, First Series*. EETS, s.s. 17. London: Oxford University Press. [*ÆCHomI*]

Colgrave, Bertram, and R. A. B. Mynors. (eds.) 1969. *Bede's Ecclesiastical History of the English People*. Oxford: Clarendon Press.

Cook, Albert S. (ed.) 1900. *The Christ of Cynewulf*. Lndon: Ginn and Company.

Crawford, S. J. (ed.) 1922. *The Old English Version of Heptateuch*. EETS, o.s. 160. rpt. London: Oxford University Press, 1969. [*Hept* (*Gen, Exod, Lev, Num, Duet, Josh, Judg*)]

Fernández-Cuesta, Julia, and Sara M. Pons-Sanz. (eds.) 2016. *The Old English Gloss to the Lindisfarne Gospels: Language, Author and Context*. Anglia Book Series 51. Berlin/Boston: Walter de Gruyter.

Finnegan, Robert E. (ed.) 1977. *Crist and Satan: A Critical Edition*. Waterloo, Ontario: Wilfrid Laurier University Press.

Forshall, Josiah, and Frederic Madden. (eds.) 1850. *The Holy Bible, containing The Old and New Testaments ... by John Wycliffe and his Followers*. Oxford: Oxford University Press.   [WycEV, WycLV]

Fowler, Roger. (ed.) 1972. *Wulfstan's Cannons of Edgar*. EETS, o.s. 266. London: Oxford University Press.   [*WCan*]

Fulk, Robert D., Robert E. Bjork, and John D. Niles. (eds.) 2009. *Klaeber's Beowullf and the Fight at Finnsburg*. Toronto: University of Toronto Press.

Godden, Malcolm. (ed.) 1979. *Ælfric's Catholic Homilies, Second Series*. EETS, s.s. 5. London: Oxford University Press.   [*ÆCHomII*]

Godden, Malcolm, and Susan Irvine. (eds.) 2009. *The Old English Boethius*. 2 vols. Oxford: Oxford University Press.

Gollancz, Israel. (ed.) 1895, rpt. 1958. *The Exeter Book*. Part I: Poems I–VIII. EETS, o.s. 104. London; rpt. New York: Kraus Reprint, 1988.

Harsley, Fred. (ed.) 1889. *Eadwine's Canterbury Psalter*. EETS, o.s. 92. Lndon; rpt. New York: Kraus Reprint, 1975.   [*PsGlE*]

Hecht, Hans. (ed.) 1900. *Bischof Waerferths von Worcester Uebersetzung der Dialoge Gregors des Grossen*. Bib. ags. Prosa 5. Leipzig: Georg H. Wigand.   [*GD*]

Holt, Robert. (ed.) 1878. *The Ormulum*, with the Notes and Glossary of R. M. White. 2 vols. Oxford: Clarendon Press.   [*Orm*]

The Holy Bible, 1611 Edition. King James Version. Nashville: Thomas Nelson Publishers, 1993.   [*AV*]

The Holy Bible. Revisd Standard Version. 1881–1885 and 1901. revised 2nd ed. of the New Testament, 1971; London/New York: Oxford University Press.   [*RSV*]

Irvine, Susan. (ed.) 2004. *The Anglo-Saxon Chronicle. A Collaborative Edition*. Vol. 7, MS. E. Cambridge: D. S. Brewer.   [*ChronE*]

Kimmens, Andrew C. (ed.) 1979. *The Stowe Psalter*. Toronto Old English Series 3. Toronto: University of Toronto Press.   [*PsGlF*]

Krapp, George Philip, and Elliott van Kirk Dobbie. (eds.) 1931–53. *The Anglo-Saxon Poetic Records, I–VI.* London: Routledge and Kegan Paul, New York: Columbia University Press. [*ASPR* (*Beo, GenA, GenB, Met, PPs*)]

Kuhn, Sherman M. (ed.) 1965. *The Vespasian Psalter.* Ann Arbor: University of Michigan Press. [*PsGlA*]

Lindelöf, Uno. (ed.) 1909. *Der Lambeth-Psalter, I. Text und Glossar.* Acta Societatis Scientiarum Fennicae, Tom. 35, No. 1. Helsinki. [*PsGlI*]

Madden, Sir Frederic. (ed.) 1847. *Laȝamon's Brut, or Chronicle of Britain.* 3 vols. rpt. New York: AMS, 1970. [Laȝ]

Miller, Thomas. (ed.) 1959–63. *The Old English Version of Bede's Ecclesiastical History of the English People.* EETS, o.s. 95, 96, 110, 111. London: Oxford University Press. [*Bede*]

Morris, Richard. (ed.) 1869. *Early English Alliterative Poems.* EETS, o.s. 1. rpt. London: Oxford University Press, 1934. [*Pearl, Cleanness, Patience*]

–. 1873. *Trinity Homilies* in *Old English Homilies, Secod Series.* EETS, o.s. 53, pp. 2–219. London: Oxford University Press. [*TrinHom*]

–. 1874. *Cursor Mundi.* EETS, o.s. 57, 59, 62, 66, 68, 99, 101. rpt. London: Oxford University Press, 1961. [*Cursor*]

–. 1874–80. *The Blickling Homilies of the Tenth Century.* EETS, o.s. 58, 63, 73. rpt. London: Oxford University Press, 1967. [*BlHom*]

–. 1886. *Lambeth Homilies, Vespasian A.xxii Homilies,* and *Sawles Warde* in *Old English Homilies, First Series.* EETS, o.s. 29 and 34, pp. 2–159, 217–244, 245–267. rpt. New York: Greenwood Press, 1962. [*LambHom, Vesp.A.Hom, SWard*]

O'Brien O'Keeffe, Katherine. (ed.) 2001. *The Anglo-Saxon Chronicle. A Collaborative Edition.* Vol. 5. MS. C. Cambrige: D. S. Brewer.

Powell, Frederick Y. (ed.) 1883, 1965. *Corpus Poeticum Boreale: The Poetry of the Old Northern Tongue,* 2 vols. New York: Russell & Russell.

Roberts, Jane. (ed.) 1979. *The Guthlac Poems of the Exeter Book.* Oxford: Clarendon Press.

Roeder, Fritz. (ed.) 1904. *Der altenglische Regius-Psalter.* rpt. Tübingen: Max Niemeyer, 1973. [*PsGlD*]

Rosier, James L. (ed.) 1962. *The Vitellius Psalter.* Cornell Studies in English 42. Ithaca: Cornell University Press. [*PsGlG*]

–. 1964, 1966. "Instructions for Christians", *Anglia* 82: 4–22 and 84: 74. [*Instr*]

Sedgefield, Walter J. (ed.) 1899. *King Alfred's Old English Version of Boethius.* rpt. Darmstadt: Wissenschaftliche Buchgesellschaft, 1968. [*Bo*]

Sievers, Eduard. (ed.) 1892, 1966. *Tatian.* Paderborn: Ferdinand Schöningh.

Skeat, Walter W. (ed.) 1887, 1871, 1874, 1878 [rpt. 1970]. *The Gospel according to Saint Matthew, Saint Mark, Saint Luke and Saint John.* Darmstadt: Wissenschaftliche Buchgesellschaft. [*Li, Ru1, Ru2, WSCp, WSH, Mt, Mk, Lk, Jn*]

–. 1881–1900. *Ælfric's Lives of Saints.* EETS, o.s. 76, 82, 94, 114. London Oxford University Press. [*ÆLS*]

Sweet, Henry. (ed.) 1871–72. *King Alfred's West-Saxon Version of Gregory's Pastoral Care.* EETS, o.s. 45, 50. London: Oxford University Press. [*CP*]

Thorpe, Benjamin. (ed.) 1844. *Aelfric. Sermones Catholici* in the Original Anglo-Saxon with an English Version. 2 vos. London: Ælfric Society. rpt. Hildesheim/Zürich/NewYork: Georg Olms, 1983.

Vigfusson, Gudbrand, and F. York Powel. (eds.) 1965. *Corpvs Poeticvm Boreale. The Poetry of the Old Northern Tongue from the Earliest Times to the Thirteenth Century.* 3 vols. Now York: Russell & Russell.

Weber, Robert, and Roger Gryson. (eds.) 1969, 2007. *Biblia Sacra, Iuxta Vulgatam Versionem.* Stuttgart: Deutsche Bibelgesellschaft.

Wildhagen, Karl. (ed.) 1910. *Der Cambridger Psalter.* Bibliothek der angelsächsischen Prosa 7. rpt. Darmstadt: Wissenschaftliche Buchgesellschaft, 1964. [*PsGlC*]

Wordsworth, Iohannes, and Henricus I. White. (eds.) 1973. *Nouum Testamentum Latine.* London: The British and Foreign Bible Society.

Studies

Atkin, Tamara, and Francis Leneghan. (eds.) 2017. *The Psalms and Medieval English Literature. From Conversion to the Reformation.* Cambridge: D. S. Brewer.

Baugh, Albert C. and Thomas Cable. 1993, 2002 (5th ed.). *A History of the English Language.* London and New York: Routledge.

Campbell, Alistair. 1959. *Old English Grammar.* Oxford: Clarendon Press.

Donoghue, Daniel. 1987. *Style in Old English Poetry*. New Haven and London: Yale University Press.

Ellegård, Alvar. 1953. *The Auxiliary Do: The Establishment and Regulation of Its Use in English*. Stockholm: Almqvist & WIksell.

Engblom, Victor. 1938. *On the Origin and Early Development of the Auxiliary Do*. Lund Studies in English 6. Lund: C. W. K. Gleerup.

Farr, James M. 1905. *Intensives and Reflexives in Anglo-Saxon and Early Middle English*. Baltimore: J. H. Furst.

Gaaf, Willem van der. 1904. *The Transition from the Impersonal to the Personal Construction in Middle English*. Anglistische Forschungen 14. Heidelberg: Carl Winter.

–. 1929, 1930. "The Conversion of the Indirect Personal Object into the Subject of a Passive Construction", *English Studies* 11: 1–11 and 12: 58–67.

Gelderen, Elly van. 2000. *A History of English Relative Pronouns. Person, SELF, and Interpretability*. Amsterdam/Philadelphia: John Benjamins.

Hasty, J. Daniel. 2012. "We might should oughta ake a second look at this: A syntactic re-analysis of double modals in Southern United States English", *Lingua* 122.14: 1716–1738.

Hiltunen, Risto. 1983. *The Decline of the Prefixes and the Beginnings of the English Phrasal Verb*. Turku: Turun Yliopisto.

Kemmer, Suzanne. 1993. *The Middle Voice*. Typological Studies in Language 23. Amsterdam/Philadelphia: John Benjamins.

Kilpiö, Matti. 1989. *Passive Constructions in Old English Translations from Latin*. Mémoires de la Société Néophilologique de Helsinki 49. Helsinki: Société Néophiloogique.

Kitson, Peter. 2002, 2003. "Topography, Dialect, and the Relation of Old English Psalter-Glosses (I) and (II)", *English Studies* 83.6: 474–503, 84.1: 9–32.

Lanout, G. J. McBeath. 2015. *The Present Participle as a Marker of Style and Authorship in Old English Biblical Translation*. diss. University of Toronto.

Los, Bettelou. 2005. *The Rise of the To-Infinitive*. Oxford and New York: Oxford University Press.

Matsuse, Kenji. 2015. "May the Force be With You", *Kiyo* (Faculty of Education, Kumamoto University 64: 77–84. [in Japanese]

Mitchell, Bruce. 1985. *Old English Syntax*. 2 vols. Oxford: Clarendon Press.

Moore, Samuel, rev. by A. H. Marckwardt. 1969. *Historical Outlines of English Sounds and Inflections*. Michigan: Ann Arbor.

Moore, Samuel, and Thomas A. Knott. 1975. *The Elements of Old English*. Michigan: Ann Arbor.

Mossé, Fernand, tr. by J. A. Walker. 1952, 1968. *A Handbook of Middle English*. Baltimore and London: Johns Hopkins.

Mustanoja, Tauno. 1960. *A Middle English Syntax*. Mémoires de la Société Néophilologique de Helsinki 23. Helsinki: Société Néophilologique.

Nurmi, Arja. 1999. *A Social History of Periphrastic DO*. Mémoires de la Société Néophilologique de Helsinki 56. Helsinki: Société Néophilologique.

Ogura, Michiko. 1982. "Functional Equivalents of DEAD", *Senshu Jmbun Ronshu* 29: 129–149.

–. 1984. "*Cwyst þu* as an OE Interrogative Equivalent", in: Shigeru Ono, et al (eds.), *Studies in English Philology and Linguistics in Honour of Dr. Tamotsu Matsunami* (Tokyo: Shubun International), 14–33.

–. 1986a. *Old English 'Impersonal' Verbs and Expressions*, Copenhagen: Rosenkilde and Bagger.

–. 1986b. "Old English 'Impersonal Periphrasis', or the Construction 'Copula + Past Participle' of 'Impersonal' Verbs", *Poetica* 23: 16–52.

–. 1987. "Latinisms? — Constructions chiefly found in the Gospels, the Psalter, and the Hexateuch", *Tsuru University Review* 27: 53–67.

–. 1988a. "*Ne ondræd þu* and *Nelle þu ondrædan* for *Noli timere*", *Studies in English Literature*, Notes in English Number (1988): 87–101.

–. 1988b. "Direct or Indirect? — *þæt* as a Quotation Indicator", in: Kinshiro Oshitari, et al (eds.), *Philologia Anglica. Essays Presented to Professor Yoshio Terasawa on the Occasion of his Sixtieth Birthday* (Tokyo: Kenkyusha), 88–105.

–. 1988c. "*Him self, Him selfe,* and *Him selfa* — A Reflexive Pronoun + Uninflected or Nominative *Self* —", *Studia Neophilologica* 60: 149–157.

–. 1989a. *Verbs with the Reflexive Pronoun and Constructions with SELF in Old and Early Middle English*, Suffolk: Boydell & Brewer.

–. 1989b. "Simple Reflexives, Compound Reflexives, and Compound Forms of 'Refl/non-Refl Pron + *Self*' in Old and Middle English", *Studies in Medieval English Language and Literature* (The Japan Society for Medieval English Studies) 4: 49–72.

–. 1990a. "What has Happened to 'Impersonal' Constructions?", *Neuphilologische Mitteilungen* 91: 31–55.

–. 1990b. "*Me cwæð* in MS. Cotton Claudius B. iv.", *Notes & Queries* 235.2: 152–154.

–. 1991a. "*Cweðan + To* + Dative of Person", *Neophilologus* 75: 270–278.

–. 1991b. "Is Indirect Discourse Following OE *Cweðan* Always in the Subjunctive Mood?", *English Studies* 72: 393–399.

–. 1991c. "*Displese yow* and *Displeses yow*: OE and ME Verbs Used Both 'Impersonally' and Reflexively", *Poetica* 34: 75–87.

–. 1991d. "Periphrases with OE and ME Verbs", *Chiba Review* 13: 37–70.

–. 1991e. "Simple Verbs, Prefixed Verbs, and Verb-Particle Combinations in OE and EME Works", *Studies in Modern English* (Modern English Association) 8: 55–73.

–. 1992. "Why is the Element Order *To Cwæð Him* 'Said To Him' Impossible?", in: Matti Rissanen, *et al* (eds.), *History of Englishes* (Proceedings of the ICEHL 6) (Berlin: Mouton de Gruyter), 373–378.

–. 1993a. "On the Development of English Verbs of Motion — with special reference to the medieval period", in: Kazuo Araki, *et al* (eds.), *Aspects of Modern English* (*Studies in Modern English: Special Issue*) (Tokyo: Eichosha), 128–145.

–. 1993b. "Verbs prefixed with *Ofer-* and *Under-* in OE and ME", *Chiba Review* 15: 19–49.

–. 1993c. "Notes: *Shal* (*not*) *mowe*, or Double Auxiliary Constructions in Middle English", *Review of English Studies* 44: 539–548.

–. 1994. "Grammatical Choice in Old and Early Middle English", in: Francisco Fernández (ed.), *Current Issues in Linguistic Theory*, Vol. 113 (Proceedings of the ICEHL 7) (Amsterdam: John Benjamins), 119–129.

–. 1995. "The Interchangeability of Old English Verbal Prefixes", *Anglo-Saxon England* 24: 67–93.

–. 1996a. *Verbs in Medieval English. Differences in Verb Choice in Verse and Prose*, Berlin: Mouton de Gruyter.

–. 1996b. "OE *Habban* + Past Participle of a Verb of Motion", in: M. J. Toswell and E. Tyler (eds.), *Studies in English Language and Literature. 'Doubt wisely': Papers in Honour of E. G. Stanley* (London: Routledge), 199–214.

–. 1997a. "The Variability of OE *Faran* and *Feran*", in: Terttu Nevalainen and Leena Kahlas-Tarkka (eds.), *To Explain the Present. Studies in the Changing English Language in Honour of Matti Rissanen* (Helsinki: Société Néophilologique), 149–162.

–. 1997b. "On the Beginning and Development of the *Begin To* Construction", in: Jacek Fisiak (ed.), *Studies in Middle English Linguistics* (Trends in Linguistics. Studies and Monographs 103.) (Berlin: Mouton de Gruyter), 403–428.

–. 1997c. "Three Features of Old English Verbs of Motion", *English Studies* 78: 316–329.

–. 1998a. "On Double Auxiliary Constructions in Medieval English", in: Jacek Fisiak and Akio oizumi (eds.), *English Historical Linguistics and Philology in Japan* (Berlin: Mouton de Gruyter), 229–236.

–. 1998b. "The Grammaticalisation in Medieval English", in: Jacek Fisiak and Marcin Krygier (eds.), *Advances in English Historical Linguistics (1996)* (Trends in Linguistics. Studies and Monographs 112.) (Berlin: Mouton de Gruyter), 293–314.

–. 2000. "'*Gewat* + infinitive' and '*Uton* + infinitive'", *Neuphilologische Mitteilungen* 101: 69–78.

–. 2001a. "Verbs used Reflexively in Old and Middle English — A Case of the Syntactic Continuity and Lexical Change", *Neuphilologische Mitteilungen* 102: 23–36.

–. 2001b. "Verbs of Emotion with Reflexive Constructions", in: Christian Kay and Louise Sylvester (eds.), *Lexis and Texts in Early English: Studies presented to Jane Roberts* (Amsterdam: Rodopi), 203–212.

–. 2002a. "Verbs of Motion in Laȝamon's *Brut*", in: Rosamund Allen, Lucy Perry and Jane Roberts (eds.), *Laȝamon. Contexts, Language, and Interpretation* (King's College London Medieval Series 19.) (London: King's College), 211–225.

–. 2002b. *Verbs of Motion in Medieval English*, Cambridge: D. S. Brewer.

–. 2003a. "*Have do make* and *have do and make* in the *Paston Letters*", *Notes & Queries* 248.1: 8–10.

–. 2003b. "The Variety and Conformity of Old English Psalter Glosses", *English Studies* 84: 1–8.

–. 2003c. "'Reflexive' and 'Impersonal' Constructions in Medieval English", *Anglia* 121.4: 535–556.

–. 2003d. "Anticipatory *Do*", in: Masanori Toyota (ed.), *Studies in Modern English: The Twentieth Anniversary Publication of the Modern English Association* (Tokyo: Eichosha), 251–264.

–. 2004a. "*The King Liked Pears:* a Choice rather than a Change", *English Language and Linguistics* (The English Linguistic Society of Korea) 18: 213–228.

–. 2004b. "Lexical Comparison between the Glosses of the *Vespasian Psalter* and the *Regius Psalter*", *Poetica* 62 (Special Issue: Medieval English Dialectology, ed. Michiko Ogura) (Tokyo: Yushodo), 17–36.

–. 2005a. "Words of Emotion in Old and Middle English Translations of Boethius' *De Consolatione Philosophiae*", in: Akio Oizumi, Jacek Fisiak and John Scahill (eds.), *Text and Language in Medieval English Prose: A Festschrift for Tadao Kubouchi* (Studies in English Medieval Language and Literature 12.) (Frankfurt am Main: Peter Lang), 183–206.

–. 2005b. "Some Variable Features of Negative Elements in Old English Psalter Glosses", in: Marcin Krygier and Liliana Sikorska (eds.), *Naked Wordes in Englissh* (Medieval English Mirror 2.) (Frankfurt am Main: Peter Lang), 1–26.

–. 2006a. "Element Order Varies: Samples from Old English Psalter Glosses", in: Michiko Ogura (ed.), *Textual and Contextual Studies in Medieval English: towards the Reunion of Linguistics and Philology*. (Proceedings of the 1st International Conference of the Society of Historical English Language and Linguistics.) (Frankfurt am Main: Peter Lang), 105–126.

–. 2006b. "Old English Preverbal Elements with Adverbial Counterparts", in: Hans Sauer and Renate Bauer (eds.), *Beowulf and Beyond: Papers presented at the IAUPE Medieval Symposia in Munich and Vancouver* (Frankfurt am Main: Peter Lang), 101–117.

–. 2006. "Old English *Metres of Boethius:* how to accept the *Consolation of Philosophy* in an alliterating form", *English Language and Linguistics* (The English Linguistic Society of Korea) 22: 173–195.

–. 2007a. "Old and Middle English Verbs of Emotion", *Poetica* 66 (Special Issue: Emotions, chiefly in Medieval and Early Modern English, eds. Hans Sauer and Michiko Ogura) (Tokyo: Yushodo Press), 53–72.

–. 2007b. "OE *Agan to* Reconsidered", *Notes & Queries* 252.3: 216–218.

–. 2008a. "Old English Verbs of Tasting with Accusative/Genitive/*Of*-Phrase", *Neophilologus* 92.3: 517–522.

–. 2008b. "Variant Readings in the Two Manuscripts of the West Saxon Gospels: MSS CCCC 140 and CUL Ii.2.11", in: M. Amano, M. Ogura and M. Ohkado (eds.), *Historical Englishes in Varieties of Texts and Contexts* (Proceedings of the 2nd international conference of the Society of Historical English Language and Linguistics) (Frankfurt am Main: Peter Lang), 109–120.

–. 2008c. "Negative Contraction and Noncontraction in Old English", *Neuphilologische Mitteilungen* 109.3: 313–329.

–. 2008d. "Periphrastic Renderings and their Element Order in Old English Versions of the Gospels", *Studia Anglica Posnaniensia* 44: 63–82.

–. 2009. "The Interchangeability of the Endings *–ende* and *–enne* in Old and Early Middle English", *English Studies* 90.6: 721–734.

–. 2010. "Old English Verbs with the Genitive Object — A Doomed Group?" in Yoshiyuki Nakao, Michiko Ogura and Osamu Imahayashi (eds.), *Aspects of the History of English Language and Literature* (Proceedings of the 3rd international conference of the Society of Historical English Language and Linguistics) (Frankfurt am Main: Peter Lang), 53–69.

–. 2011a. "The Grammaticalisation of Old English Imperatives *weald* and *loca*", *Notes & Queries* 58.1: 10–14.

–. 2011b. "Interpreting the Differences in Signification among Historically-Based Dictionaries of English", in J. M. Toswell (ed.), *Constructing a World. One Word at a Time: Papers on the Dictionary of Old English Project. Florilegium* 26 (Canadian Society of Medievalists, 2009), 67–83. [Published 2011]

–. 2012a. "Verbs with Personal, 'Impersonal' and Reflexive Constructions in Medieval English", in Jane Roberts and Emma Volodarskaya (eds.), *Language, Culture and Society in Russian/English Studies* (King's College, London), 14–24.

–. 2012b. "Words and Expressions of Emotion in Medieval English", *Studies in Medieval English Language and Literature* 27: 1–38.

–. 2013a. "Ambiguity in Old English", in Michio Hosaka, Michiko Ogura, Hironori Suzuki and Akinobu Tani (eds.), *Phases of the History of English* (Frankfurt am Main: Peter Lang), 161–178.

–. 2013b. *Words and Expressions of Emotion in Medieval English*, Frankfurt am Main: Peter Lang.

–. 2013c. "Verbal Periphrases in Old English", in Jukka Tyrkkö, Olga Timofeeva and Maria Salenius (eds.), *Ex Philologia Lux: Essays in Honour of Leena Kahlas-Tarkka* (Mémoires de la Société Néophilologique de Helsinki 110) (Helsinki: Société Néophilologique), 57–79.

–. 2014. "Two Syntactic Notes on Old English Grammar: (1) OE *beon/ wesan* + present participle, (2) OE *standan* as a Copula", in Michiko Ogura (ed.), *Aspects of Anglo-Saxon and Medieval England* (Frankfurt am Main: Peter Lang), 105–134.

–. 2016. "Compound Reflexive as a Metrical Filler, or *Self* in *Himself* as an Alliterating Element?", *Studies in English Literature*, English Number 58: 77–95.

–. 2017. "What really happened to 'impersonal' and 'reflexive' constructions in Medieval English", in Jacek Fisiak, Magdalena Bator and Marta Sylwanowicz (eds.), *Essays and Studies in Middle English* (Frankfurt am Main: Peter Lang), 141–162.

–. 2018 (to appear). "Indirect Object or ex-Dative with or without *to* in the Earlier and Later Versions of the Wycliffite Bible".

Rissanen, Matti. 1967. *The Use of ONE in Old and Early Middle English*. Mémoires de la Société Néophilologique de Helsinki 31. Helsinki: Société Néophilologique.

Standop, Ewald. 1957. *Syntax und Semantik der modalen Hilfsverben im Altenglischen 'magan', 'motan', 'sculan', 'willan'*. Bochum-Langendreer: Heinrich Pöppinghaus.

Terasawa, Yoshio. 1974. "Some Notes on ME *gan* Periphrasis", *Poetica* 1: 89–105

Traugott, Elizabeth C. 1972. *A History of English Syntax: A Transformational Approach to the History of English Sentence Structure*. New York: Holt, Rinehart and Winston.

Visser, Frederik Th. 1963–73. *An Historical Syntax of the English Language.* 3 Parts, 4 Vols. Leiden: Brill.

Wahlén, Nils. 1925. *The Old English Impersonalia. Part I. Impersonal Expressions Containing Verbs of Material Import in the Active Voice.* Göteborg: Elanders Boktryckery Aktiebolag.

Index of Examples

Studies in English Medieval Language and Literature

Edited by Jacek Fisiak

www.peterlang.com

www.ingramcontent.com/pod-product-compliance
Lightning Source LLC
Chambersburg PA
CBHW030248100426

42812CB00002B/356

*9 783631 756805 *